Mary Brainard

Memorial Pictures of War and Peace

Mary Brainard

Memorial Pictures of War and Peace

ISBN/EAN: 9783337009175

Printed in Europe, USA, Canada, Australia, Japan

Cover: Foto ©ninafisch / pixelio.de

More available books at **www.hansebooks.com**

OF

WAR AND PEACE.

BY

MARY BRAINARD.

PUBLISHED BY THE AUTHOR.

ROCKFORD, ILLINOIS:
GAZETTE STEAM BOOK AND JOB PRINTING HOUSE.
1873.

Entered according to Act of Congress, in the year 1873, by

MARY BRAINARD.

In the Office of the Librarian of Congress.

TO

The Nevius Post, G. A. R.,

ROCKFORD, ILL.,

THIS BOOK

IS

Respectfully Dedicated

BY

THE AUTHOR.

	PAGE.
THE McNIELS.	
THE HOMESTEAD.	9
THE MEETING-HOUSE.	32
THE DESOLATE.	40
WAR.	45
THE HOSPITAL.	80
HOME.	113
YEARS AGO.	
RETROSPECTIVE.	131
LUCRECE,	146
WITHOUT GOD.	154
THE WILDERNESS.	170
PEACE,	186
LOVE AND YOUTH,	194
LOYAL.	196
THE LOST,	198
THE SINGER.	202
ROLL ON.	206

THE McNJELS.

THE McNIELS.

THE HOMESTEAD.

I SING of what the days have been,
   And what the days will be ;
I sing of life and life's reward
   As it appears to me.

I sing of sorrow sanctified,
   Of trial overpast ;
I catch the meaning as I can
   Of every shadow cast.

As I go out in harvest time,
   To glean among the sheaves,
I try to learn the tracery of
   The sunlight on the leaves.

I analyze, at eventide,
   The thoughts that go and come,
When the eye is fixed on vacancy
   And the dreamer's lips are dumb.

I have only taken one little leaf,
   Where the forest of dead leaves fall,
And sent it afloat on the ocean of life—
   God guard it, who guideth all!

An Eastern river, flowing down,
Doth glide past hamlet, woodland, town,
Doth widen, deepen, all the way
From upland spring to ocean bay.
Along that winding river bank

A turnpike winds, and wild and rank
The woods that skirt a reedy tarn,
Give place to field and grain-filled barn;
On either side that turnpike lay
The farm of farmer Ethan Day.

Four decades, like a transient dream,
Have come and gone: so short they seem,
That all betwixt that day and this
Might vanish into nothingness;
But what a world of weal and woe,
Of birth and death-pangs come and go,
And leave no trace while passing by,
On fair green earth or azure sky.

O'er acres broad of leveled grain,
The binders toiled with might and main;
For though the pulse of earth seemed still,
With distant growl, behind the hill

Storm forces crouched, till upward crowd
The purple peaks of thunder-cloud.

Upon his fence leaned Ethan Day,
And wiped great beads of sweat away
From sun browned brow and iron-gray
That hung above; "Comes mighty fast:
A good share must be wet at last,"
He muttered, as he turned his eye
Now on the field, now on the sky.

Just then two travelers came down
Along the road from Beacontown,
Whose Highland garb and bonnet loose
Told of the land of Burns and Bruce;
Old Ethan's brow unbent a smile,
"Come bear a hand and help awhile."
The lads o'erlept the fence, where they
Wrought side by side with Farmer Day,

THE HOMESTEAD.

Awkward somewhat, but ready will
Supplying lack of use and skill.
The sheaves were garnered, and the rain
Fell, but fell not on Ethan's grain.

The weeks of harvest passed away:
Still on the farm of Farmer Day
The brothers found employ.
Corn, golden-eared, was gathered in;
And ripened fruit, in many a bin,
Was heaped with grateful joy.
Well pleased was Ethan with the sense,
The sterling worth, intelligence,
His Scottish lads displayed.
Well pleased were James and Dan McNiel
To find a place where they could feel
So home-like, while they stayed.
Thus lingering on, from year to year,
Through summer's toil and winter's cheer,

Seed-time and harvest days,
The brothers grew at last to be
Part of the farmhouse family,—
So well they learned its ways.

Where, willow-fringed, the river flowed,
Beside the winding valley road;
Where, sloping back, the sunny hill
Merged into meadows green and still,
Enclosed in orchard, like a wood,
The old, deep-gabled farmhouse stood.
It caught the earliest sunlight gleams;
Looked wierd and castle-like in beams
Of moonlight through the trees—
So hushed, retired, that all day long
Your heart kept beating to the song
Of birds and humming bees.

Upon the parlor wall there hung,
And still doth hang, two faces, young

THE HOMESTEAD.

And radiantly fair;
Twin daughters of the house were they—
The hope, the pride of Farmer Day,
The darlings of his care.
Belle was a beauty — deep and bright,
And ebon as the starless night
Her laughter-loving eyes,
In flush of health, in dancing curl,
A woven charm enwrapped the girl—
An ever glad surprise.
But Nellie, with the self-same grace
Of feature, form, and fair young face,
Like starlight to the sun,
Shone with a pale, retiring grace,
A brow that shamed at honest praise---
A meek, lone-hearted one.

I said the lads were pleased to stay,
Till months and seasons passed away,

And blythe the old house grew;
For healthful hearts, unvexed by pride,
Made merry round the ingleside
Long winter evenings through,
Till, by and by, as age crept on,
The good man, looking o'er his lands,
Feeling the need of clearer head
And younger hands,
Did just as I would do:
He halved his farm in equal parts
And gave his daughters where their hearts
Had fixed in instinct true.

Together in the farmhouse wide,
A few short years they did abide.
Then James and Belle marked out a spot
For home on their apportioned lot,
Beyond the dairy spring,
So near that little toddling feet

Could cross the way, and voices sweet
With blended notes could sing.

And thus it was, bewildered, wild
With loneliness, I stood a child
Beside my mother's grave---
A birdling, cast with wounded wing,
To earth, a timid, helpless thing.
One hand was stretched to save,
Was gently laid upon my head,
And gentle-toned the voice that said,
" Poor child! all, all alone."
God bless him! Good it was to feel
The strong right arm of James McNiel
Around the orphan thrown;
And good--so good that even now
I feel its soft touch on my brow,
Though decades intervene.
The kindly touch that banished pain,

That fair face, mingling with the train
Of fevered fancies wildered, vain,
That come and go and come again,
And clothe my world of dreams.

Another shadow seems to stand
From out the past; in waxen hands,
Spring violets folded, half unblown,
The earliest, opening alone
Within the forest dell.
Clouds floating slowly, far and high—
Like dream-land, floating silently—
Sunshine and shade alternately
Upon a casket fell.
A mother, lily-like and pale,
Tears falling through a mourning vail
Upon her earliest born,
A baby-face, with half-shut eyes
Blue as the sky, the glad surprise

Of breaking smile at morn,
Then, empty arms, and hungered hearts,
And life all tasteless for a while;
Then strivings vain, and loving arts,
To raise the wonted smile.

As fair a maid was Annie Lee
As one might ever hope to see;
As fair a maid, as fond a wife,
As ever crossed the deeps of life,
Or dared, from girlhood's sunny bay,
The storm-tracked billows of the way.
A wife and mother, blessed, she found
Life, for a while, all blessing-crowned;
And then, the tempest of the night
Swept all her loved ones from her sight:
And she, dismantled and alone,
A wreck upon the rocks was thrown.

Into the merry sunshine, went
Her merry, winsome boy;
Back to her heart his ringing shout
Brought message of his joy;
The glow of pride still in her eye.
His good-by kiss still warm;
Without one warning chill, or sigh,
A lifeless, stiffening form.
The drowned, with fair curls dripping wet,
And lips all blue and cold,
And dreadful staring eyes, death-set,
Borne back into her fold.
Then, ere the moon had waned six times,
And six times filled her horn,
The father by his dead boy slept;
And she, bereaved, forlorn,
Did plead, in vain, with God to die.
She might not lay life's burden by,
She might not rest in death; she bore
The mother's promise, not before

That germ of life awoke to day,
So, conscious only of her woe,
Months dragged like years away.

And then the snows of Christmas fell,
Like God-gifts, silently,
And earth enrobed in spotless white,
And bending shrub and tree,
Looked pure as heaven-born holiness --
As spotless charity!
Unwelcomed e'en by mother-love,
Came Annie's blue-eyed boy,
Yet fair enough to change the wail
Of sorrow into joy;
"O, bear the babe away, *away*,"
Thus wailed her pleadings wild,
"No more shall heart of mine entwine
About another child!"
Half-crazed, the woman dwelt alone,

We who were children then
Did fear to pass her door, as one
To pass a wild wolf-den;
Then into Nellie's empty arms,
And into Nellie's heart,
The babe, deserted, crept and found
A faithful mother's part.

'Twas Sabbath twilight, and we strayed
Where James his home foundation laid,
The children, Belle and I.
How o'er the hills of long ago,
Comes back the silvery, silent glow
Of moon, new-risen, red and low,
Comes back the solitary cry
Of whippoorwill from o'er the stream,
The shimmering white vibrating beam
Athwart the wavelets flow,
That dashed like play upon the sand,

That washed the pebbles from the strand.
Again I hear the low,
Deep music of that solemn hour,
And feel the weird enchanting power
Of river, rock, and dreaming flower,
That dreamed so long ago.
The wee ones frolicked, hand in hand,
Among the stones along the sand,
But I, a child of ten,
Felt—for those few eventful years,
Had deepened by the weight of tears—
Almost a woman then.
Among the timbers framed and planned
Her home to rear, the wife did stand;
My little fingers clasped her hand—
Was it the moonlight, like a vail,
Upon her cheek and lips so pale?
Was it some silent, hidden grief,
That shook her like the blasted leaf?
She sank in weakness to the ground,

And I, I clasped my arms around
My more than mother, till
She calmer grew, and, with a smile,
Bade me go join the play awhile.
But I, with childish will,
Crept in the shadow of a tree,
Unheard to hear, unseen to see;
For, O, I feared some day,
The same sad destiny that gave
My precious mother to the grave,
Would snatch her too away.

Deeming herself unnoticed now,
With hand hard pressed upon her brow,
She murmured, "It will rise at last,
But not for me its shadow cast.
My feet shall ne'er return or roam,
Or cross the threshold of this home;
Else why this death-toll in mine ears,

THE HOMESTEAD.

And why these dark foreboding fears,
Not wont am I to be
So weak." And then her one wee child
Looked up into her eyes and smiled.
But when she called to me,
From brow was banished trace of pain,
She seemed her own bright self again.

Ope thou the scroll of fate and show,
In each home history here below,
The days of weal, the days of woe,
Doom-days and marriage bliss,
As time, with sure recording hand,
Marks this a day of peace to stand,
And that of bitterness.
Anon, a shadow cast before,
Pall-like and tinged with gloom, spreads o'er
The dial-face of love.
Anon, destruction springs to birth,

And blights the beauty of the earth,
And blots the stars above.

I may not tell how many days
Passed in their old accustomed ways,
I know that dim and high,
And waning in the eye of morn,
The ghost-like moon did glide forlorn
Toward the western sky.
I know the rose-vine clambering o'er
Its lattice by the shaded door,
Gave promise then of bloom—
Now backward leaning from its stay,
Burdened with blossoms fell away—
Upon that day of doom.
I know, 'twas planned the night before,
To take the skiff and row us o'er
To Alden's field, where, well we knew,
Strawberries in abundance grew.

THE HOMESTEAD.

We older children, with the freight
Of coming joy, could scarcely wait
The slow-winged hours,
Until our tiny, well-filled boat
Of happy hearts was set afloat,
Along the bank of flowers.

We all, that morning, seemed to be
The embodiment of gaiety.
Now one would seize and ply the oar,
Now shout to grandma on the shore;
The bird-like warble of our song
Echoed the river lengths along.
And need I tell you as I pass,
How, down among the bending grass
We bent the scarlet fruit to pull,
Till sun was low and pails were full.

We drew toward home, I scarce can tell,
By some mad, playful prank of Belle.

The boat o'erturned, and young and old
Were struggling in the water's fold.
I know I sank, and rose and sank,
Then for a space 'twas all a blank,
And then, upon the river bank
I lay, and saw as in a dream,
The children rescued from the stream.
I saw, borne downward by tide,
One wild face 'neath the waters hide,
With hands up-reaching as to cling
To life, a flashing marriage ring.
Then blackness settled like a pall,
And nothing more can I recall :—
Yes, I remember faces white
And set as death ; and all that night,
By ghostly torch and beacon light,
The neighbors dragged the river's bed
In fruitless searching for the dead ;
And I remember days of pain,
When even speech seemed task-like, vain,

THE HOMESTEAD.

And one who never smiled again.
Another stroke was never laid
On that new home, beneath the shade
Of the old homestead, doubly dear,
We dwelt together year by year.

Did I not say the child of ten
Was scarce a child, that even then
She questioned life with deepest view,
As one who reads its mysteries through;
As one who, up in the early dawn,
Goes out upon an upland lawn,
Finds all the dew of morning gone;
Yet, doubtless, girlhood's opening rose
Had richer tints and sweeter bloom,
The summer charm that romance throws
Like wreaths of ivy o'er the tomb;
Doubtless, new rooted in the soil,
The plant of hope took form above;

For where are desert fields of toil,
Too barren for the plant of love,
All that was over long ago;
Not of myself this tale is told;
Of richer lives, with hope aglow;
Of young hearts, folded in the fold
Of guardian care—parental pride—
That grew to beauty by my side.

Of Helen, now, the motherless,—
The one wee nestling left behind,
With not one trace of mother's face,
With not one trait of mother's mind,—
Tall, fragile, fair, the slight form swayed
Like fern leaf in the forest glade:
She seemed the graceful mountain maid
Of Scotia—far off land.
James often said his mother there
Had those gold-lighted locks of hair,

When last he saw her stand
Framed in their cottage door ; and she
Her last good-by had wept and kissed :
Then saw the dear home picture melt
Into the morning mist.
From her, he said, came all that quaint
Deep earnestness of soul,
That made the maiden half a saint ;
Timid, and yet so bold ;
That trust in God's unwearied care ;
That inward pureness born of prayer.

I told you of twin sisters fair
Within the walls of home.
I said, with life-song half unsung,
That one so radiant and so young
Had vanished like the foam
That tips the crest of ocean wave,
Windrocked above her unknown grave.

But o'er the hillside where she roamed
In girlhood's glee and pride ;
And when they met to worship God
Around the ingleside,
In morning hymn of praise,
At evening's sacred close,
Was one as like her as the bud,
Half opened, to the rose ;—
But this was Nellie's girl : oh, well,
To name her as they called her, Belle.
For friend and villager who stood
To bless her as she passed their door,
Felt, in the rush of memory's flood,
The welling of a nevermore.

THE MEETING-HOUSE.

A mile away, and yet in sight,
  Clasped by its grove of evergreen,

THE MEETING-HOUSE.

With heavenward finger, pointing white
  And high above its leafy screen,
Our meeting-house—the house of God—
  Surrounded by God's acre old,
Where we with reverent footsteps trod,
  Where the sweet gospel news was told.

Before its altar, infant brows
  Grew radiant with the mystic seal;
Beside its altar, marriage vows
  Gave answer to the merry peal
Of bridal bells; and through its gates
  The old, the young, the rich, the poor,
Brought hither by their mourning mates,
  Were laid to rest forevermore.

Rememberest thou the spirit-tide
  That swept the churches like a flood?
Rememberest thou three years therefrom
  The nation was baptized in blood?

Rememberest thou how hand in hand
   And heart to heart the churches stood,
Old feuds forgotten ; through the land
   A God-led, christian brotherhood?
Rememberest thou that Mercy's pool
   Was troubled to its center-depths
By faith and prayer man measured out,
   Divine compassion length and breadth?
Rememberest thou, like that of old,
   "A going in the mulberry trees?"
He who was wise and saw afar,
   He who could read such signs as these ;
And he whose heart had come to beat
   One with the Infinite, could tell
The arm victorious gathered strength
   Against the opposing host of hell.
The pastor heard it ;—all his soul
   With awe was filled, with wonder bowed ;
With Christ communing face to face
   He entered in the cloud.

The elders heard, and trembling hands
   Held forth the bread and wine ;
And eyes aflame with love did search
   The Oracle divine.

Lips, sealed by fear, from dumbness woke,
And light on clouded vision broke ;
The Cross, long trailing in the dust,
Grew radiant with wreaths of trust.
The loved, the wayward, the unwarned,
Heard, at the solemn midnight hour,
Their names in tones of pleading power.
New altars rose at eve ; at morn
New prayers were prayed, and old set form
Was broken like the winter's chain,
When Spring by love and light doth reign.
Proud hearts grew strangely burdened and oppressed ;
Great thoughts of God broke in upon their rest;
Life and Life's deep enigmas pressed them sore—

The solemn echoes of a nevermore—
Till, loathing sin's caresses, free and fond,
A longing rose for purer life beyond.

The startled host of Satan knew it well,
   And strengthened their defences as they might.
The red saloon, with eye malignant, fell
   To claim its prey, the votary of the night :
And strangely frequent grew the midnight dance ;
   And sweet young voices prayed and prayed to go—
Making of death a long eternal choice—
   And to the voice of warning answering no.
These times of choosing, how they ebb and flow,
   Like tidal-wave upon the lives of all;
These times of choosing, how they come and go,
   And pass beyond redemption or recall !
O, saddest of all memories at the close,
   That youth's bright warp be filled with threads of
                                    [sin,

When, 'neath the weary shuttle, grows and grows
    The web of destiny, "The might have been!"

That short December day drew to a close;
    Persistently the great snow crystals fell.
The moon at full, but veiled by storm, arose,
    Rose dimly, as a vision or a spell.
'Twas God's own day; and like a beacon light
    Shone the far windows of our bowered church;
Long tints of flame athwart the snow-drift white,
    On leafless branches of the silver birch,
On laden evergreen and hazel bowed,
    And on the faces of the gathering crowd
Lay like a benediction golden, bright.

Around the blessed altar, bathed in tears,
    Gathered the tried ones, who, for long, long years,
Had borne the burden of His sacred cross,
    And counted, for His sake, all things but loss.

As vows of new-pledged fealty arose,
  New peace descended, filling all desire—
The same baptismal blessing that of old
  Crowned each disciple with its tongue of fire.

The white and red, each striving to prevail
On Helen's cheek. Beside the altar rail
She stood in timid boldness, quiet, meek
And spirit-bound, till gathering strength to speak:
"I ever loved the Master, Christ, but this,
This day I wed my soul to Him and His."
But oh, the contrast! By the dear child's side—
She fair and pure enough to be favored bride
Of heaven—stood one so shrunken and so old;—
A world of wasted fire to ashes cold
Burned down; a world of fevered dreams;
A world of anguish with its death-mark seems
Lettered upon that brow in lines of care,
And written in the folds of time-bleached hair;

But from the 'wildered eye all madness swept
Or melted into meekness as she wept.
We sang, "There is a fountain filled with blood;"
And poor crazed Anna in that healing flood
Redemption found; found reason's long dimmed
[light
Rekindled; found the long woeful night
Fled; with recreated peace complete,
Sat down a meek disciple at His feet.

Need I to tell of other hearts and lives
   That found new birth amid repentance there?
How faith awoke the soul to glad surprise?
   How God gave answering pardon to their prayer?
Need I to tell how swift descending grace
   Awoke the desert's desolate repose?
How wilderness did bloom, and barren place
   Did bud and blossom like the opening rose?
Enough to say, some harps in heaven, new strung,

Caught in that hour the pean of his praise.
Enough to say of those disciples young
   Strong-handed reapers rose for after days.

THE DESOLATE.

A room so bare, so desolate,
   So comfortless, it seems
Some weird enchantment, where the soul
   Lies struggling with dreams.
Wildly the winds of winter shook
   The broken shutters there;
Black shadows wrapped the broken roof,
   And hid the broken stair.

The mocking fire-light's fitful glow,
   Like fevered visions came,
Now sinking into shadow low,
   Now rising into flame;

But on the sufferer's blood-red cheek,
   And in her burning eye,
The flame dimmed not that drank her life
   And drained its fountain dry.
And ever in the mournful hush
   Of wind and winter rain,
Came tear-filled tones and broken prayers,
   And bitter moans of pain.
Then changed the winter's rain to sleet :
   Then changed the sleet to snow,
And all was black as grief above,
   And all was white below.

Beside the couch, with shrouded eyes
   And white lips washed by tears,
Sat Nellie, by the wasted friend
   Of girlhood's happy years.
"I know," the woman moaned ; "I know
   I cast my child away ;

I know whose kind arms sheltered him;
  Who watched his childish play.

Ah, well know I he felt no care
  Or motherhood but thine,
And that his fair young brow would shame
  At any claim of mine:
And yet through all these wandering years
  My lone life claimed its child,
With wilful hunger unappeased
  And nature's yearning wild.

For in his eyes I saw the glance
  That won my love of yore;
And on his brow, the brow I lost,
  In sorrow's nevermore.
Now, as I gaze from shore to shore,
  As lift the death-mists dim,

THE DESOLATE.

My heart *will* claim this latest boon—
   One filial kiss from him."

The flush of fever faded slow ;
   The cold white death-look came
From out the vast unseen, and fell
   Athwart the stiffening frame;
As, cold and white, the risen light
   Pushed back this night of storm ;
Yet colder grew the snow clad earth,
   And still in death the form.

A boy stood by the couch of death,
   And held an icy hand
As one who treads a hopeless maze
   He may not understand ;
As one whose welcome-song hath changed
   To grief's farewell refrain ;

Whose careless, happy-hearted past
　　Will never come again.

A boy stood by an open grave;
　　But less he wept for this
Than for the living and the lost,
　　The vanished dream of bliss:
Yet ever from his kindred's tomb
　　There seemed to rise a tone—
To rise and echo through his heart,
　　Alone, alone, alone.

Then back to old home scenes he went
　　Of schoolboy tasks and joy,
With manhood's chill upon his heart
　　For aye—no more a boy:
As one from vales of summer green
　　By swift ascent should rise

And stand upon the snow-clad Alps,
   Beneath the stormful skies.

Yet, strangely sweet, one bird of spring
   Forever went and came :
The song-bird love, kept trilling out
   His playmate Helen's name :
And strangely sweet the star of hope
   Smiled down from winter skies ;
Forevermore the hue it wore
   Of Helen's summer eyes.

WAR.

On the wonderful mount of Vision
   The prophet of Israel stood,
And beheld, through ages and ages,
   Earth deluged with tears and blood ;

But, beyond this, did Beulah, the golden,
   In the arms of the Orient lay—
The sun-lit, the land of the morning,
   The jeweled millennial day.

When the Prince of Peace hath descended
   And ignorance, want and pain
Led captive, shall grace the chariot
   Of the Victor's triumphant train ;
When the sword to the useful ploughshare
   Shall yield in the mighty change,
And the lamb and the love-tamed lion
   Through forests of plenty shall range.

Not now, O toiler, life-weary—
   The seer's vision was far ;
But over the fields of the future
   Has arisen the Morning Star :
There is God in the earth's upheavings.
He shall turn, He shall overturn ;

He speaks, and the war fires kindle ;
   He permits, and they blight and burn.

Somewhere on the green earth's bosom
   Is a place for thy slumbers blest,
Where the wicked shall cease from troubling,
   And the weary shall be at rest ;
When the eye that is tired of seeing,
   And the heart that beats painful and slow ;
When the lips that are wearied of asking,
   And the feet that no further can go
May return to the silence of nature,
   To mingle again with the dust ;
May sleep till the trump of Jehovah
   Shall awaken the evil and just ;
May sleep, to awake new-created,
   When the risen Messiah shall reign,
And earth shall be wedded to heaven,
   And love be the links of the chain.

Yes, you had heard of battle rage;
And, musing o'er historic page,
Thought the vast thought of former age:
Yes, and the July signal gun
Had told you tales of freedom, won
By men who followed Washington;
And some you, even knew, were slain
On Buena Vista's bloody plain.—
But was not this another word
Your peace-accustomed ears now heard,
Though it at first to you did seem
As dimly distant as a dream?
Yet in the rising of the storm,
How, one by one, your fears took form.
E'en in the quiet winter eves,
E'er strife had turned the dreaded leaves,
Fast locked within the book of fate,
And pointed out the desolate;
A forecast shadow seemed to fall
Around your future so unknown;

Your wakened spirit felt its thrall,
    And life took on a mournful tone.

One sat within the firelight glow
    And read the daily signs of strife;
And you kept turning to and fro
    Your leaves of life.
He read the heated, madd'ning thought
    Of Southern despots, passion-stirred;
You, as your busy fingers wrought,
    Prayed o'er the bitter words.
The glow of noble purpose rose,—
    You saw it in his kindling eyes—
And, woman-like, took up the load
    Of sacrifice :—
Such sacrifice as he could know,
    Who firmly up Moriah trod,

Swept sight and selfishness away,
   And left you heart to heart with God.

'Twas early morn—an April day;
A Sabbath silence brooding lay
Upon the field, upon the wood,
Upon the hill side where I stood.
A riverlet, with widened range,
Rejoicing in its spring-wrought change,
Sang like a soul from dungeon free
Its song of jubilee;
And, here and there, just bursting forth,
Close by the bank, close to the earth,
Sprang tiny blossoms into birth;—
Men call them snow-drops, though, 'tis true,
They wear a tinge of crimson hue—
As might a pure cheek flush to flame,
And crimson at a deed of shame;

And, looking upward as in prayer,
The early crocus everywhere :
While all the hill-slope clothed with green,
In burnished sunrise might be seen,
Like regal velvet mantle's fold,
With dandelion clasps of gold.

All night before, electric life
Flashed through the land its tale of strife ;
All night before, wild pulses beat
Along the crowded city street
That echoed to the tramp of feet,
Men, white with anger, clasped their hands
And mutely stood, as one who stands
And feels the gathering of woe,
And knows not whence to meet the blow :
All that night long, wrestling with fears,
Was woman's pillow drenched with tears ;

Our country farmhouse far and lone,
Had not received its lightest tone.

That Sabbath morning, still and sweet;—
What did I dream! of gathering feet,
Where force opposing forces meet?—
What did I dream! of mad'ning rage
That wrote with blood-marks history's page,
And drenched our holy heritage?
Northward, I heard a rumbling tone,
Like distant thunder's smothered moan;
Can it be storm? I glanced on high—
No cloud lay on the smiling sky;—
Again, like distant lion's roar,
Up from the west it came once more,
Louder and clearer than before—
Then o'er the mountains far away,

Upon whose wooded summits lay
The rosy sunrise of the day.
My heart stood still with awe at first,
And then the truth upon me burst;
And then I wailed, accursed, accursed
The hand that kindles into life
The death-fires of this awful strife!
Then bent I humbly to the sod;
My heart-trust questioned—questioned God.
In vision saw I, far as ken
Could reach, long ranks of risen men,
With stern-set brows, and eyes aglow,
With steady tramping footfalls slow,
March on to meet the risen foe;
And ever o'er their faces fell
A misty, vail-like, fare-thee-well.

I said, as faded out the view,
"Land of my heart, my heart is true;

These be thy sons, I love thee too;
They die for thee—what can I do?
I stood in spirit by a field—
    A field whereon were spread
Long swaths, as by a reaper mown,
    The dying and the dead:
I seemed to see the fading out
    Of hope in many an eye;—
I seemed to hear the broken wail,
    The agonizing cry.

I stood in spirit by a tent,
    And I heard the conflict roar;
And fast as they carried the dead away,
    The bearers came back for more.
I was treading the length of a long, dim ward,
    Where, worn to weeping, lay
The bearded man and the wan-faced boy,
    Moaning their lives away.
And wasted arms, and cold, white hands
    Beckoned the shadows through;

And voices, hoarse with pain, wailed out—
"Woman, we die for you!"
I said within my burdened heart,
"I know what I will do."

When homeward through the fields I trod
The morning dew had left the sod;
And meadow-land and hillside lay
In warm embrace of middle day,
I passed the spring where cattle drink,
And greening willows kissed the brink—
A mirror set and framed in green,
Within whose silent depths were seen
Soft April cloudlets floating by
Above, beneath, a double sky,—

Then, in unrest, I went and stood
Beside old timbers weather-browned,
On what to us seemed holy ground;

A poison ivy winding clasped
The ruins in its serpent grasp.
" Ah, this is fate," the tempter said,
" That binds the living to the dead."
I shrank and shuddered, half dismayed,
As if a hand was on me laid;
Then turned reluctantly and slow,
And crossed the stepping-stones below.

From lifted sashes reached me there
The low deep tones of fervent prayer—
Such earnest pleading as the soul
Holds 'wildering grief in firm control,
And speaks in calm unfaltering trust
To Him whose hidden ways are just.
I saw two brothers hand in hand
And heart to heart together stand,
With locks in vivid noon-bright glow,—
One golden brown, one white as snow.
In both I saw the wedded truth

Of thoughtful prime and finished youth,
That dwelt in noble manhood now,
Like halo round each care-lined brow.

One woman knelt apart, alone,
And, now and then, a smothered moan
Repressed, a chill, a sudden start,
Bespoke the mother in her heart.

I saw one fair young face repose
Upon the window-sill, the rose
All faded from her lips, and tears
More bitter than her youthful years
Had ever known, kept running o'er
Her hand and dropping to the floor.

A youth and maiden, side by side,
With something new, a dash of pride,
A wild, adventurous fervor took

Weird form in willfulness of look.
Hugh seemed to fret, as I have seen
A high-bred horse for action keen,
As thoughts like these, his pulses stirred—
This is a day for deeds, not words.
I saw their eyes meet, and a smile
Struggle with awe in both awhile:
O children, thought I, never were
Such deeds as actions born of prayer.

One, unimpassioned, stood; the task
Of questioning all overpast;
Upon the other was the glow
Of indecisive feeling's flow:
I, to myself said, he will go.
He glanced at Helen, slow and true
Rose tears into his eyes of blue.
Barred by strong will, these drops of pain
Fell back into their depths again.

WAR.

I said, full well, these signs I know,
Down to the front this man will go.

The day drew slowly to its close,
Another work-day sun arose.
Few were the words we said,
Too deeply surged the tide of thought,
The near unknown, with peril fraught,
On every moment meaning wrought:
We walked as they who tread
With bated breath all silently
Along the brink of destiny.
A pallor, born of pain, made white
The dear house-mother's cheek,
Men looked into each other's eyes
The words they would not speak.
A little waiting and suspense
Through towns and scattered farms,
Then came the marshaling of men,

The clarion call, "To arms!"
Then over all the sanctified
Birth-pangs of sorrow roll,
And love unselfish, brought to birth
The hero in each soul.

Beside the turnpike, just half-way
Between the farm and village, lay,
By laurel-bordered moss o'ergrown,
Smooth as a floor, the half-way stone.
'Twas Wednesday afternoon, I think,
The sun just tipped upon the brink
Of Alden's forest, all agleam
And lined with gold the thread-like stream,
That ringed the rock with gentle flow,
And crossed the pasture-land below.

Half hidden by the hazel bough,
Half hidden by the maple wood,

With hand hard pressed upon his brow,
The farmer stood—
He saw no sight, he heard no sound,
Oblivious to all around—
All light on inner vision cast,
As one whose temple is the past,
Who waiteth by the altar, pale,
To sacrifice within the vail,
Where echo of an outer word
Its solitude hath never stirred,
And never sacred seal or book
Hath opened to another's look.

A foot-fall, and another stands
Beside him, and a brother's hands
Upon his shoulder fell.
"I sought you, James, because to-day
Somewhat I have to you to say,
A dream to you to tell:

Our Highland home I saw last night,
Just as it faded from my sight,
Folded in mountain mist.
Our own dear mother, true and good,
As in her cottage door she stood
When she her lads had kissed;
But, O! her locks like winter grown,
And tear-light in her dear eyes shone,
Her broken voice was mournful now
As wind-sigh in the forest bough.
I thought our mother, weeping, said:
'The battle-plain is heaped with dead—
O, let not Jamie go!
The toll of death is in mine ear,
I see the crowded trenches near;
The long lines bend and break and flee,
Like dead leaves on the wind-swept lea;
I see the white lips of the slain
Washed by the fall of midnight rain—
O, let not Jamie go!'"

The younger brother raised his head:
"I, too, have dreamed a dream," he said,
With earnest, mournful tone;
"Ne'er since my love went down between
Yon banks, have I her bright face seen,
Even in dreams, till now;
Yet, surely, with her own fair brow,
By yonder hazel wood,
All blithe and bonny as of old,
And folded in the star-flag's fold,
My bride before me stood—
Stood silent—yet I heard my name
Wind through a funeral refrain;
And this I heard, 'We'll meet again,
Beloved, upon the battle-plain!'

"Now, brother, lay I on thy heart
My heart's last hope and care—
My Helen, with our mother's look,

Her sunny eyes and hair;
She never knew another home,
And may it never be,
Within my faithful brother's ward
She feel the need of me."

Two lads, side by side, in the wide field wrought,
One silent, and seemingly wrapped in thought,
The other, his restlessness scarcely restrained,
Half in anger and half ashamed:
"Ho, beauties!" laughed he, and released
His oxen from the plow,
"Part you and I, my pets, in peace;
Another hand must guide you now,
Other than I shall reap this field,
Must place upon your necks the yoke,
For, till the cursed traitors yield,
I'll never take another stroke.
Come, Hugh, 'tis time for you and I
To bid this quiet farm good-bye!"

WAR.

"O, yes," was answered, "as you say,
My heart has said good-bye all day;
But, if I go, then you must stay."
"I stay! well, that is good! Why, Hugh,
Should not I fight as well as you?"
"You are the younger, Bruce, you know;
One is enough of us to go,
But if the war should be prolonged,
And other calls should come,
If I should fall—" Said Bruce, "Enough!
Think you I'll lag at home?
I'll tell you how to settle this:
Stand here upon the green,
Which is the better of the two
Is very quickly seen;—
I've almost felt, since Sumter fell,
As I could lift a ton,—
The one shall have the earliest chance
Who brings the other down."

With quiet smile upon his face,
Hugh spread his arms for the embrace.
He was a young athlete in strength;
Before he knew it, all his length
Bruce lay upon the ground,
Then, rising, burst in angry tears,
And, without glancing round,
Ran off, and hours and hours that day
The boy could not be found.

Through the length and breadth of the North
                                         [land, then
Was seen the uprising of earnest men.
Not alone from the hive-like city streets,
Where life like a throbbing artery beats,
From the factory's din, and the workshop's roar
Did the throng of our patriot soldiery pour;—
No,—he with the sun-brown upon his brow,
Left in the furrow that spring his plow.

And gave, in the hour of its first alarm,
His life as a shield from the nation's harm.
Then names were written that rent aside
The lover's pledge to his promised bride;
Then names were written that did destroy
The mother's right in her first-born boy;—
Names were written and prayers were prayed,
That common folks into heroes made.

I remember that twilight, like fate folded down,
The day when equipped for a neighboring town,
Our boys stood ready to go.
A foreboding faintness crept into my heart,
As if life from our life was rending apart,
But we would not answer them, No!
They went from our midst, and we knew that
[when

So we sat and talked of the direful need,
And each to herself and the others agreed
To repress all weeping when our soldiers start
And send them away with a cheerful heart.

.

Twelve short hours! To-morrow night
Must they stand in the gleaming Capitol's light—
Stand as a guard in the cause of right.
Only twelve hours for the sad good-bye,
With its rush of thought, and its quick reply,
Crowding upon the memory:—
Twelve night hours, but no eye closed,
Hours for rest but no head reposed.
Then petitions ascended to the God of Heaven,
Then garments were folded and keepsakes given,
For we knew when the starlight gave place to the
[dawn.
The first volunteers from our midst would be gone.

And then they *were* gone, and we must remain,

Treading the tread-mill of duty the same.

I remember those weeks, with their death-peril
[fraught,

When the 'wildered brain reeled with intenseness
[of thought,

When the earliest blood-sprinkle, falling before

The storm, stained thy pavement, O, mad Balti-
[more!

How up from the Southland came the shrill battle
[cry,

How down from the North rang defiant reply,

How the hearts of both rivals with love-longing
[burned,

As their eyes on the Capitol-city were turned :—

White as death, I remember, the spring lilies came:

I remember the tulips, with blood-hues aflame;

The long, lonesome twilight; the lonesomer morn;

The pitying whispers that swept through the corn;

Remember the soul-wearing days of suspense,

Waiting for tidings;—remember, at length,

When the worn missive came from the warm [soldier's heart,

How over and over each read them apart.

I remember our sickness of soul at the tramp

Of the boys who brought back their dead comrade [from camp;

How we covered his casket with blossoms and [tears;

How we wept as one weeps when the promise [of years

Hath departed:—remember the grief-wailing sent

O'er the brow of the boy who had died in his [tent;

Remember the brother, with white, tearless face,

Who said, "I am going to fight in his place!"

All this, and much more, o'er the shore-sand is [cast,

Like the wrecks of a storm, by the tide of the [past.

It was early midsummer. From morning a cloud

Hung away to the South, like the folds of a [shroud,

Or sulphur-smoke rising, as black as the tomb,—
The north-sky all sunshine, the southern all [gloom,—
We saw the faint flashing, as lightning at play,
We heard the low growl, as a lion at bay:
We said, "A storm riseth,"—ah! little we knew
The storm sweeping over our army of blue.

We were watching and waiting; our Bruce was [away
At the nearest town, seeking the news of the [day;—
The hours dragged slowly, ten, eleven, and one,
The thought of retiring was mentioned by none.
We knew the boy tarried for tidings—we knew
There was work at the front, and we shuddering [drew
Our breath, when his footstep was heard in the [hall.
He entered, his eyes red with weeping:—"'Tis all
Lost! we are driven and scattered and slain,
A cowardly rabble is all that remain."

All lost! was the burst of our bitter surprise—
All lost! was the burden of grief-choked replies

"Let us pray," said the father; and then in his
[prayer
"God save our rent nation—God help our despair
God stay the black tide of destruction—God keep
Our Capitol safe from its desolate sweep!
Arise, O, Most Holy! come swift to our aid!
O, Christ, let this fearful rebellion be stayed."
Then the after-pang, with its sickening pain,
Where dread sang ever her sad refrain,
Of the trampled dying and the blood-drenched
[plain
Of the hopeless wounded in the mad retreat,
And the frantic hurrying rush of feet.
A whole week passes, we cannot hear;
Face to face with harrowing fear—
Then came the death-list; our boys were in
The roll of our wounded and missing kin—

Heading the death-list was James McNiel,
Wounded and left on the conquered field :—
Leading the charge, like a soul-brave man,
He fell ere the shameful retreat began.
And was that all? O, how much to guess
In the troubled dream of the fatherless.

I had heard the old clock in the kitchen strike
[four,—
I had counted its strokes, for the night hours
[seemed long,—
I saw from my window the day-star hang o'er,
The dimmest, the faintest gray signal of dawn.
Like an angel's chant, fell on my half-dreaming
[ear,
Or a rising *Te Deum*, the grove-warblers' song ;
Now I lay, with a dim, undefined sense of pain
Like a woe on the heart, like a weight on the
[brain:
I heard a faint footfall, a half-smothered cry:

A warm rain of tears on my neck and arms fell,
And, sobbing as deeply as if she would die;
She lay on my bosom, our brave-hearted Belle:
"O, Rachel!" she cried, " I so long for the day—
O, Rachel!—our Bruce—he is now far away!
Was it foolish and wrong, that I let him bind
My lips to silence—will the blame be mine
If he never returns?—he could not endure
The tears of parting; and fixed and sure
He had given his name: and, O, far away
Will my brother be on the coming day!"
She shivered with grief;—"O, the long, long night;
Will it never, O, never again be light?"—
But she slumbered at last, with long grieving sigh
Of an infant so weary no more it can weep:
Thanks, thanks, to the balm-laden angel of sleep.

So another was gone, and closer we drew;
And smaller and smaller, our home-circle grew.

Then came the harvest: that year in the grain,
Unheeding the sunshine, unheeding the rain,
We girls helped to gather the bountiful yield,
And bring forth the corn, golden-eared, from the
[field.

A missive from Bruce—alas! how delayed—
A missive of sorrow: he earnestly prayed
Help for Hugh, worn and wounded, and day
[after day
In the ward of the hospital wasting away;
And then in a postscript from the suffering one,
In lines scarcely legible—Rachel must come.

As one upon his journey stayed—
Longing to go and yet delayed,—
All that long summer through;
This single purpose kept in sight,

Deeming that sometime in the night
Would come a call to do.
Now, as the warrior-heart in all
Its fibre feels the bugle-call,
A living impulse thrilled me through,
As if a voice said, "Rise and do!"
And I at roll-call made reply,
On eve of battle, "Here am I!"
Yet one heart-broken maid replied:
"Dear Rachel, I shall never 'bide
At home, for, surely, by his side
My right it is to stand;—
Entreat me not, I would not stay
If angel-hands should bar the way,
Or human voice command!"

"Can this be a dream?" said I to my heart;
As the laboring cars, with their living freight,
Onward, onward into the dark,

Passed over the bounds of my native State;—
"Can this be a dream—this parting to-night,
This rending of home-life for sacrifice?"
Then I turned to the girl, with her hand in mine
And looked for an answer into her eyes,—
Looked for an answer: such a world of woe
Up through those patient orbs gleamed through
That I whispered, "Helen, O, Helen, weep!"
And the poor white face to my shoulder drew.

"Are you going down to the front, my child?"
The tones were rough, but the eyes were kind:
"You bear the look of a girl I knew,
In the dear old village I left behind,"—
'Twas the voice of an officer sitting near.
I glanced in his face, it was honest and true;
An armless sleeve lay across his breast,
And a Captain's badge on his army blue.

"Yes, down for a brother who is nigh to death—
At Manassas wounded!" I quietly said;
He sighed, "There my good sword-arm was left,
But many a better man lay dead."
Then Helen started, as from a dream:
"Perhaps, my father you may have known—
Captain McNiel, of the Seventeenth;—
That he fell, was all that was ever shown."

" Are you his daughter? Why, I knew him
 [well;
He stood at my right in the same brigade;
He was bravely cheering his comrades on,
When the heaviest charge of the day was made.—
'Twas a great, grand sight; ere the word was
 [given,
As I glanced mine eyes along the line;
There were many a look uplift to heaven,
And many a life-pulse throbbed, like mine.
I saw him again, in the wild retreat,—

Under a shot-riven tree he lay,
But the smile on his lips was as calmly sweet
As one who a lover has chanced to meet,
And I knew he had peacefully passed away.
I was bleeding and faint, we were sorely pressed;
Most of the wounded were left to die:—
O, many a beautiful life went out
Under that sulphurous, cloud-wrapped sky.
You never, *never* will understand,
Though I sit and talk till my head were gray,
One half of the woe of this war-cursed land;
And I ask of the Lord, that you never may.
I shall go to the front, though my work is done
In the ranks; of my good right arm bereft,
I shall answer my roll by the couch of pain,
I shall war with a different enemy—death."

Swiftly over the war-bound we sped;
Wasted vineyards and unrept fields,

Homes deserted, and hearth-fires dead—
The ghastly harvest rebellion yields.
Sometimes, by the wayside, a Union flag
Hung from a farmhouse, faded and dim;
Sometimes, in the door-way, a scowling face
Gave index of traitorous heart within;—
And ever, the gleam of the camp-fire light.
And ever the sentinel, mute and grim.

THE HOSPITAL.

"Here, matron!" spoken in hurried tones,
As we stood in the hospital hall;
"Here are the friends of No. nineteen,"
And that was all:
The surgeon, a man with cheery face,
A prompt but a quiet tread,
Went back to his office; in a moment more,
The matron stood by us instead.

One of those women who always drift,
  By a natural instinct, where
Are wanted the tones of a softer voice,
  The touch of a tenderer care;—
One of those women who never flinch,
  Whatever the heart may feel;
Who into the warp of love can weave
  A woof of the sternest steel.

"Come into my room a moment, dear,
  'Till the nurse of his ward I call."
I was glad, for Helen was cold and white:
  And she trembled as if she would fall.
She entered the room with the soldier-nurse:
  "It is well you are come," he said.
"I was sadly afraid, with the best of our care,
  Your friend would be dead;"
For more than a week he has called and called,
  In bewildered, delirious tone;

For Helen,"—and a smile that was half a tear,
   In the eyes of the soldier shone.
"If Helen has come, I think he will rest;
   But if," he said, with a sigh,
"We cannot ward off this homesickness,
   I'm afraid he will die."

What was one soldier?—a hundred lay
   Tossing with feverish dreams of home,
All through the long night wishing for day,
   Pleading and praying for some one to come;
Come ere the life-chord asunder be riven,
   Come ere the golden bowl broken shall be,
Come that the kiss of farewell may be given,
   Ere the tried soul launch out on eternity's sea.

What, though he lay with his hand in her hand?
What, though he pillowed his head on her breast;
Though the blissful hush of a great deep calm

To the slumber of infancy lulled him to rest?
Though he wakened with new life coursing his
⠀⠀⠀⠀⠀⠀⠀⠀⠀⠀⠀⠀⠀⠀⠀⠀⠀⠀⠀⠀⠀⠀⠀⠀[veins;
And said, "I shall live," in blissful surprise;
The man on his right and the man on his left
Hid under their blankets their tear-dimmed eyes.

What was one soldier? A hundred lay
Suffering to death within my call;
But Helen bent over him day by day:—
He was her all.
Love is selfish, and cares for one;
Separates one from among the crowd;
Reareth its altar for sacrifice;
Forever over that altar is bowed:
Nor doth it matter if thousands fall,
If homeward the light of my life shall come;
Nor if a thousand hearts shall starve,
If plenty abide in my home.

There is something better than self-bound love,
Forever revolving around its sun;
Gathering honey and hoarding it up,
And pouring it into the lips of one;
Better dilute it a little, and spread,
So that it cover a broader space;
And give to the famished, the half unfed,
A morsel—a taste.
O, the heart of a man is a selfish thing,
   And the love of a woman is even more;
Like the long armed ivy, 'will cling and cling,
   Till it crushes the oak that it clambers o'er.—
Thank God that the death of a Christ could rend
   The veil of the Holy and Most Holy place!
Thank God the heart of a Christ can clasp
   The whole wide world in a love embrace!

May I call you mother? And a queer smile
                                      [spread,
   Half fun, half sorrowful joy.

"Only fourteen was his age," he said;—
  Just an overgrown boy.
I sat by his sick couch half of the night;
  All efforts for rest were vain;
His cheeks were thin, and his lips were white,
  And he moaned like a child in pain.
"May I call you mother?" (I had held his hands
  And soothed him with all of my art;
I suppose it reminded the suffering boy
  Of his mother's hand and heart:)
"Yes, call me mother; but tell me first
  Of your own dear mother at home:—
Why, Willie, you're fit for nothing but school;
  What could have possessed you to roam?"
"O, a great war meeting was held that night,
  And speeches were made in our town:
They said the Southerners fired our forts,
  And our star-spangled banner hauled down.
You know the story of launching the ship;—
  I thought I could push a pound."

"I believe you have pushed a good many pounds;
  But had you no brothers to go?
And where was your father? Did he not refuse?"
  He sorrowfully answered, "no;
I have only my mother—the rest are all dead—
  And she—oh, I'd rather not say;"
And the great tears rose to the poor lad's eyes
  And rolled from his white cheek away.
Yes, even now, when the overflow
  Of the past with its sorrow and joy
Returns in the swelling of memory's flood,
  I wonder, "O, where is my boy!"

"Will you write me a letter?" said a wounded
                                        [man,
  With his great black eyes on me;
"You see, they have ruined my writing hand;
  'Twas a sorrowful joke to me;
For letters, you know, are a soldier's life,

And she writes like a parson, my excellent wife.
"I should like to show you our nice little home;
Flowers, we've a garden full :
Wife, she has a knack of crowding the yard
With everything beautiful.
That rose, you know, with the dew on its leaves,
The fragrance was just the same
As the vine she trained over our portico :—
Such a rush of home memories came,
That I closed my eyes, and you thought I slept,
But I lived it all over again."

"Children—why, yes, we have three, my boy,
   And Lilly, and baby Grace;
And a nobler boy you never will find
   Than I left at the dear old place;
And Lilly is just a little woman,
   And the babe has the sweetest face.

"But, for the children I'd send for her—

She's the steadiest nerves and eye—
I was half killed once, but she brought me round,
Though the doctors all said I would die.—
I tell you the boys would be sure of one friend,
If *my* wife was here to stand by."

So I wrote a letter to that excellent wife,
Just as he dictated, word for word,
A real love letter—how I honored the man—
He remained through the war; and I heard
That he met all his darlings face to face—
The boy, and Lilly, and baby Grace.

"Well, Rachel," said Helen and Hugh one day,
"You seem to have found your sphere;
The furlough has come, shall we go away
And leave you here?"
In the first sweet balm-days of early spring,
With health-light and hope in his eye;

And the rest of a heart giving love for love,
   They bade me good-bye.
And I knew, when over the threshold of home
   The mornings of April should play,
The friends of the maiden would garland her brow,
   And give her away.
I also knew, that the morn of love
   Would bring with it parting pain;
When the soldier lover must gird his sword,
   And off to the war again.
Those days of struggle, when death and life
   Stood bearing the palm between;
Those days of trial; of strife on strife,
   Like a wierd panoramic scene—
Passing, passing, with their couches white,
   And their long, hushed wards of pain;
Where eyes were dimming into the night,
   Where life-visions wax and wain.

Praying the Father to silence doubt;
   Gazing with strengthened sight

Into the opening fields of bliss
    And heavenly light;
Wiping the damp off the cold, white brow,
    For the march is ended, and the day's
                                            [don
Laying the knapsack and canteen by,
    At the set of sun;
Folding the pictures and keepsakes up,
    And sending them home.

Backward and forward the war-tide beat,
    Like a wave on the wild seashore:
Names unnoticed before, at length,
    A terrible meaning bore.—
Shiloh, Bethel, and Donelson,
    Vicksburg and Malvern Hill,
Each with their quota of wounded men
    The vacated cots to fill.
I look in my diary, November tenth,
    Eighteen sixty-two,—

The first enlisted are veterans now,
  But the ranks are filling anew.
The Northmen arise at the President's call,
Determined to conquer or willing to fall:
A battle is fought in a western State,
The enemy driven back;
But the sick, disabled and dying men
Are scattered along the track.
Great bodies of soldiers pass through the town,
Leaving their hundreds behind;
The halls, the hotels, the churches are full;—
Wherever the eye can find
A resting-place, any and everywhere,
The convalescent and the dying are.

Dim as the light through its windows, stained,
I see in the terrible past
A great, old church—it is crowded so full;
The disabled are dying so fast.

So much to be done; and, O God! so small
The wherewith for any to do;
With that strange assemblage of patient eyes
Uplooking from every pew.
They lie on the benches, under the trees;
They rise and wander about—
Into the garden and through the gates—
And in and out;
They sit on the graves in the old churchyard
They crouch by the camp-fire light,
In their blankets folded, and the star-gleams fal
Over their faces white.
Up from the basement a racking cough
Comes, stifled by moans of pain,
Startles the sleeper at the midnight hour,
Soundeth again and again:
Heads that at home would be pillowed upon
The wife or the mother's breast,
Roll on their knapsacks from side to side,
Seeking in vain for rest;

THE HOSPITAL.

Men so prized that their native town
Were in mourning if they should die,
Close their pale lips and go up to God
Without a cry.

Great pine-trees guarding the dead men's rest,
Shivered and moaned as the wind caressed,
And the golden sunshine of winter crowned
The old church spire and the hills around;
Then, into an ocean of molten gold,
The day-god vanished, and, fold on fold,
Gathered the curtains of twilight down,
Hushing to quiet that quaint old town.

Not there the monument high, that told
The depth of the rich man's hoard of gold;
Not there the lower lots that yield
A pauper's grave in the potter's field:
It seemed, by the long lines of level mound,

As if an army had bivouac round,
Weary of marching, at evening-fall,
Waiting the morning reveille to call.

Bowed, till his head, with its iron-gray,
Prone on the grave of a soldier lay—
Bowed, till his rough coat and hardened hand
Was sprinkled over with yellow sand—
He knelt, and the deep sobs upward pressed,
Forcing their way from the strong man's breast,
He knelt, and the burning tears—ah, well!
Such tears as only a man weeps, fell.

At the head of the grave was a small cross
    [placed,
And carefully carved these four words traced,
Words of an infinite meaning to be
The sum of a life hope: "He died for me."
"Your son, I presume?" He raised his head,
Then rose and stood by my side and said:

"I will tell you stranger:—in a Northern State,

When the cause looked dark and the need was
[great,

With the clutch of the cursed rebel foe

At the nation's throat, how I longed to go;

But the frightened pleading, the dumb surprise,

That arose in my poor wife's upturned eyes!

I was very poor, but with honest hand

Had I wrung support from my rocky land;

Nothing in plenty had to me been given

But the poor man's blessing—for that thank
[Heaven!

There were boys with black eyes, and girls with
[blue,

There were youths and maidens just peering
[through

The bars that open from childhood's lane

Into the workday fields of grain,

There were toddling darlings just up to my knee,

And the four months' baby that cooed to me;

But my heart grew hot as the soldiers' tread
Went past our cottage, and my brow burned [red
For all I was fettered and burdened so,
I was half ashamed that I could not go.

Well, the draft came on, and, the worst of all,
Mine was the very first name to call.
How I reached my cottage I never could tell,
How I broke the news to my wife—ah, well!—
Somewhere I have read of a head turned white
By the sorrows that crowded a single night.
O! how swiftly the hours passed by,
As we questioned the future, Mary and I:
Mary had folded a shirt or two,
An extra pair of socks,—then drew
From the drawer a Testament, faded and gray,
The children had carried on a Sabbath day,
With a little yarn and a hank of thread:

"You will need them sorely," my poor wife said.
Then she boiled some coffee, and spread the board
With the daintiest fare of our scanty hoard;
For a moment we stood where the wee ones
[slept,
Then she threw herself into a chair and wept.
"O, darling! cannot we trust," I said,
"Who feedeth the ravens, for daily bread—
Clasping His hand, through shadows dim,
Cannot we cast our burden on Him?"

A step creaked over the frozen sill,
And a face looked in—it was Charley Hill.
Such fellows you find in most every place,
Whom the people call a very hard case,
But many good deeds had that reckless one
Mixed with the evil that he had done.

"Good morning!" he said; "you might as well
Put off that troublesome, sad farewell:—

I am going to see this Rebellion through,
And will call my name in the ranks for you.
Not a word of thanks, for cannot you see
There isn't a soul to lament for me—
Not a chick, nor a child, nor a mother to weep;—
So now go back to your bed and sleep."
But he turned, with his hand on the latch, to say
" You can pray for Charley whenever you pray.
You see I am left to my family still,
But here is the grave of poor Charley Hill.
We have scraped and gathered for more than
                                                           [year,
To lay by the money that carried me here,—
The hand of my first-born framed this wood,
But, O! by my life, if I only could,
A marble monument reared should be
For the man who has given his life for me!

Then I stood and thought, as the sunset gold
  Deepened to purple on tower and tree,

Of that old love story so sweetly told,
  Of the Man who has given His life for me.

Weary and worn to a skeleton form,
  He lay on his couch of pain:
His prayer at evening and his prayer at morn
  Was to visit his home again:

He talked of his mother, far away,
  He talked of his lonely wife;
When the fever frenzied his aching head,
  And loosened his hold of life.

We told him his feet might never again
  Walk over his native sod,
But ere long he should tread the golden streets,
  At home in the city of God.

We told him his eye might never behold
  The face of his best beloved:

He should welcome her there, by the life-river
[fair,
In the garden of beauty above.

He wept and whispered so long, so long,
So many long weary years;
And my widowed wife and my little one
Alone in the world of tears.

We shredded a lock of his long, fair hair,
The love-words were written, he said,
A great peace descended from God to his soul
And the last of his earth-trials fled.

It was only a tear, a *tear*, and it fell on the old
[man's hand,
As upon the charred and blistered sod falleth
[the sweet, sweet rain;
When his iron frame writhed in agony and forced
[the unwilling moan,
As the tempest bends the oak-tops to its autumn-
[song of pain.

It was only a tear, a tear, and the fountain from
 [whence it fell,
Since its early azure brightness, had been faded
 [by many such;
But the face had the look of an angel, the love-
 [blent magic spell,
Though washed to an ashen paleness by weep-
 [ing over much:

All its softness, and its roundness, and its rosiness
 [were gone.
I said an angel: — more like a saint's that pa-
 [tient, peaceful face;
It was autumn's ripened promise, it was twilight's
 [labor done,
'Twas a soul refined and chastened by the
 [moulding hand of grace.

I said the face of an angel, but an angel's face
 [is bright
As the full, clear, radiant splendor of the day-
 [light, golden, warm;
And this had more of the sweetness of the silent,
 [starry night,

Of a night when the moon-kissed billows are
 [resting from the storm.

I said the face of an angel, but an angel knows
 [no sin,

Has never to grapple and overcome the force
 [of a wrong desire,

To storm his own heart-fortress for the foe en-
 [trenched within,

To quench in briny tear-showers the flame of
 [a passion fire.

'Twas just at the battle's commencement, when
 [the shrill-toned, fiendish yell,

And the fire of the foe burst on them with
 [its death-hail thick and fast,

As his comrades bravely rallied, the old flag-
 [bearer fell,

Bleeding and crushed and trampled, and the
 [wheeling legion past.

Recked he of the old battalion, how the tide of
 [the conflict went?—

In that mangled frame was raging a struggle
 [of life and death,
When back from his post of honor in the
 [crowded hospital tent,
In wild, pain-wrought delirium he cursed failing
 [sight and breath.

I said that a warm tear gathered and fell on the
 [old man's hand;
As he saw with his death-dimmed vision a kind
 [face over him bent,
There seemed to glimmer above him the sky of
 [another land,
And the old home-roof of his childhood grew
 [plainer than the tent.

The kiss of an only sister swept over his cold
 [lips now,
And he knew her by the mother-look imprint
 [upon her face;
He knew her by the brown hair yet waving
 [on her brow,
Where the old fair child-lines lingered, with
 [their gentle curves of grace.

They had loved and played together in the dear
                              (days of the past,
  They had danced and sung together when life
                              (was in its May;
But, apart, they learned the lesson we all must
                              (learn at last,
  Of emptiness, of bitterness, of falsehood and de-
                              [cay.

One heart had warred with error, and at last had
                              (overcome,
  The other taken captive had become the tyrant's
                              [slave;
One had risen, ever risen, child of morning to the
                              (sun,
  The other in earth's littleness and folly dug its
                              (grave.

Hand in hand, and hearts together, in a solemn,
                              (silent fold:
  "Christ have mercy!" was the last cry of his
                              (life-thought as it fled;
Did she heed the battle tumult as it near and
                              (nearer rolled?

Did she feel the sulphur war-smoke as they
     (bore her from her dead?

God's great mercy, soldier brother, be it with
     (thee at His bar!
Jesus' presence, O, my sister! on thy mission-
     (labors shine!
Star of love that led the "Wise men," ever more
     (thy guiding star,
Crown of "Him that overcometh," bright, un-
     (fading, shall be thine.

I pray that I never again may list
 To such pitiful wailings as came,
Piercing the hush of that twilight through,
 Entering heart and brain.
After the toils of a toil-filled day,
 I lay in the quiet deep
That reigns on the border and stretches away
 Into the kingdom of sleep.—
A knock at my door—'tis the ward-master calls:
 "Can you come? there is no one but you

That can manage the woman;—'tis the wife of
(the man

Who died in the ward No. two.

You remember the man—he was buried to-day,

This morning, and now she is here,

Too late for one word, too late for one look—

'Twill unsettle her reason, I fear."

The mourner lay stretched on the vacant cot,

Where his life slowly wasted away;

She must have been poor, for her garments were
(worn,

And old, for the black and the gray

In her thin locks were mingled, and hardened
(and brown

Her hands, like a woman who washes through
(town.

On the morrow we rode in an ambulance down

Where they buried the Union dead.

The day was delightful, like June in the North,

With the bluest of sky overhead;

But the graves were unsodded, and thick yellow
[clay
Clung like paste to our feet and garments that
(day.
She gathered a handful and bore it away—
O, Love—that makes sacred the soil and the sod!
Thou banished of Eden, O, daughter of God!

July the tenth—Vicksburg has fallen!
   Not all in vain are the tears we have shed;
Back to the rear our steamships are bearing
   The sick and the wounded, the dying and dead.

.

Thanks be to God for victory given,
   Thanks, not in vain are the blood-torrents shed,
Thanks, though we wipe off the dew of the
[dying,
   Thanks, though we fold the white hands of the
(dead.

A message from home, from a mother's heart
(breaking,

As many have broken, the price of our joy—
O, bitterest anguish! O, wounded and missing!—
Asking in vain for a trace of her boy:

Asking of Bruce,—the bright-browed, the glad-
(hearted,
Our own precious home-boy, the regiment's
(pride;—
O, better, surrounded by comrades and brothers,
If he in the van of the conflict had died!

Breathe ye not a word of the prison-pen to her,
The death-line surrounding the prisoner's fate;—
Not a word of the desolate longing and waiting,
Not a word of exchanges, delayed till too late;—

Not a word of the July sun beating upon them,
Or the shelterless under a storm-shrouded sky,
Not a word of the devouring death-pangs of
(hunger:
Keep silent all this, or the mother will die!

There came a time when the surgeon looked,
Into my face and said,
"You are wearing out; you must stop and rest."
But still, with a dizzied head
And departing strength, I labored on.

   I recall it now, and it seems,
As bereft of heart and as purposeless
   As we toil sometimes in our dreams:—
The fires of a fever were draining life,
   Coming on in such slow degrees,
That I kept repeating, "I am not sick,"
   And then, on my hands and knees,
Climbed up to my little secluded room,—
   And, O! how I wept and wept;—
I cannot recall, was it night or noon,
   When I woke, or how long I had slept;
But anxious faces looked into my face,
   And nurses bent over my bed,
And I knew by the guarded, whispered tones.
   And I knew by the careful tread,

I was sick indeed—then I closed my eyes:
  I remember no more than this,
That I seemed to be drifting away, away,
  To silence and nothingness.

I again awoke, and the morning sun,
  Just lifted above the range
Of eastern ridges, looked into my room—
  But everything seemed so strange.
Through lifted sashes the early spring
  Kept flinging her rich perfume,
Rifled from peach orchards over the way,
  And the garden was all in bloom;
I gazed up dreamily into the sky,
  Where drifted a sail-like cloud,
I wondered if robins ever before
  Warbled so sweet and loud.
Some one, asleep in an easy chair,
  Leaned over the foot of my bed,—

I for a moment with memory strove,
    Then burst into weeping and said:
"Daniel McNiel, tell me quick, is it you?"
    Thank God! And my dear old friend,
Wiping the tears he fain would repress,
    Above me did tenderly bend.
"O, Daniel, how are the dear ones all?
    O, Daniel, when did you come?"—
But he placed me gently and firmly back,
    Then he sat down and talked of home.
There were lines of care I had never seen
    Crossing his brow of yore,
There were threads of silver in hair and beard
    I never had noticed before.
All at once the sorrowful truth came back,
    And the visions of sickness fled,
As one should arise and wrestle with fate,
    Go forth and bury the dead.

Ye who have mingled your songs in the light

Of the radiant summer day,
Ye who have met, on a festival night,
To revel its hours away;
Can unclásp your hands with never a thought
To deepen the light good-bye,—
Can sever the linking of gossamer life
With never a sigh!

But ye who have labored together, till months
Have lengthened themselves to years;
Ye who have trodden, hand clasping hand,
A pathway of terror and tears;—
Heart beating to heart, hand clasping hand,
Through darkness and anguish and tears:—

Ye may not sever the links of fate,
Ye may not go forth and forget;
You will find them drawing you, drawing always
Into the vale of regret;—

You will pause and listen as memory pleads,
  Plaintive and low and sweet;
And the broken thought of her bye-gone days
  She will over and over repeat.

Faces will come and look down on you
  Framed in the sunset beams,
Voices long hushed in the chambers of death
  Like a warning will ring through your dreams;
Sometimes, in the light of the moon-ruled night,
  Motionless you will stand,
And feel the blessing of voiceless love,
  And the clasp of a shadowy hand.

HOME.

The vines that clambered o'er the eaves
Were putting forth their first green leaves,

The laurel, queen of waste and wood,
Clothed in the bloom of spring-time stood,
The snow-drop in the forest dell,
The violet, the mountain bell,
Were in full bloom, as if to greet
The wanderer's returning feet;
The hazel where a child she played,
The river-border where the maid
In silent contemplation strayed,
The hillslope, green as emerald now,
Where, woman grown, she breathed her vow,
The willow-bridge, the half-way stone,
The dear church hidden by its pines,
Were all the same,—on us alone
Was wrought the ruin of the times.

Helen, the wife, now graver grown,
Had that far look within her eyes,
Of one who stands upon the shore,

HOME.

Where blends the ocean and the skies,
Though deafened by the billows' roar,
Still hopes to catch a lover's tone
Sent back in answer to her own.

The mother looked to me like one
In bridal garments, at the gate,
Who reads upon her sunset sky
Its warning—"Wait!"

A timid sadness filled the look
   That answered to our questioning eyes,
As if the Bridegroom's midnight call
   Would not surprise:—

A little struggle, ere the soul,
   Victorious in its latest strife,
With yearning love could, one by one,
   Lay down the cares of life.

And then the harvest of the year
   Was garnered; and the tassled corn
Stood full-eared, waving in the clear
   October morn.
From severed lives a new life rose—
   A babe was born;
But scarcely was there time to shred
   One ring of gold from baby's head,
For him away, when it was dead.

Before the corn was gathered in
   A deeper grave was made—
The mother of the household passed
   Into the valley's shade:
But, when upon the other side
   The gates of Eden opened wide,
A glory, piercing through the night,
   Made all our earth-home strangely bright.

Think you, with heart aflame, we read
  Of Sherman marching to the sea?
How Grant, down through the wilderness,
  Was pressing Lee?
And think you, that with heart aflame,
We gloried in the rising fame
That clothed with pride our brother's name?
Whose steady valor in the fight,
Whose firm adherence to the right—
Brave with the brave; true with the true—
Brought high reward to honor due;
For in those days of quick events
Were unknown heroes brought to view
In council halls and martial tents.

With heart aflame with joy, we heard
Of Richmond fallen; and the roar
Of cannon wrote our jubilee
From western mountains to the shore:

But sometimes mute, and sad, and pale,
  We wondered at His hidden ways;
And thought of those within the veil,
  Who saw Him face to face.

They who had quaffed the bitter cup,
  When life was hopeful, fair and bright,
And yielded all its promise up,
  To walk with Him in white;

Some earnest souls of deep desire,
  To fullest tension had been tried;
And in the flood and in the fire
  Been purified;

New, deeper lines of thought and care
  Furrowed the brow of middle life;
And men came out, where boys had gone
  Into the strife:

So, when the peals of joy rang out
   Across the land from sea to sea;
We sat and counted out the cost
   Of victory.

The past! the past!—we almost felt
   The echo of its ghastly tread;
And turned around, as if to meet
   The faces of the dead.

I said, "the days were fore-ordained,
   When war upon the earth shall cease:
Not now—though round Columbia's brow
   Be wreathed the olive branch of peace:

Not now. Across Atlantic's wave
   The wail of death and danger comes;
Where truth's upheavings lift and shake
   To their foundation, Eastern thrones.

We hear of tottering dynasties ;
    Of war's wierd wayward chance :—
For the vineyard-bordered Rhine I wept,
    And the sunny vales of France :

We hear of martyred patriots,
    And noble captains slain ;
But a thousand death-white brows I see
    Upon the carnage plain.

And louder than siege-guns roar,
    Or the long-roll's 'larum wild,
Comes the frantic mother's wail of grief
    Above her orphan child !

Alas ! for the poisoned serpent trail
    O'er that goodliest garden spot :
Alas ! alas ! for the ruined town,
    And the peasant's rifled cot.

HOME.

Roll swiftly on, O circling years,
    Till the night of sin be o'er!
Till the blood-drenched earth be purified,
    And man learn war no more.

Fold down thy curtain-folds, O Death,
    O'er the slayer and the slain!
Till One shall reign in righteousness,
    Whose right it is to reign."

I said, when heart and soul were stirred
    To meet the dim decrees of fate,
"That trifling things should never more
    A tumult in my life create.

That, having felt the pelting blast
    Of arctic storm and winter rain—
No, never, with the sun o'erhead,
    Would I complain:

But, when the tension was withdrawn,
    And daily life to common things
Sank back, think ye not that I felt,
    As keen as ever, little stings;

That buzzing, vexing, insect care
    Spun webs about me just the same,
That tripped my feet at hidden snare,
    And grieved my heart at little pain.

They handed Him the nation's coin,
    To tempt the Master;—from that day
The wisdom of our Lord's reply
    Hath never passed away.

If bow ye must to despot sway;
    If tremble at the tyrant rod;
Render to Cæsar but his own—
    The residue, to God.

A schoolboy spelleth on his coin
   Such words as these—" In God we trust."
Mother, what meaneth this thereon?
   Then to the mother's memory must
Uprise the days this was her hope—
   The cause is just.

Inscribed upon the *little* coin—
   Not on the silver or the gold—
That which the pauper's hand can reach;
   That which the infant palm can hold.

Perhaps, in ages yet to come,
   Will antiquarian clear the rust
Of ancient coin, and read thereon—
   " In God we trust:"

And from the page of history glean—
   A great Republic once was rent

By wars intestine: for these days
   This coin was meant.

All scattered up and down the land—
   In farmhouse, cot, and regal hall—
There hangeth, bound in ebon bands,
   A picture on the wall;—

Not beautiful; but honor rays
   It round with kindliness and grace;
And oft the housewife stands to gaze
   Her eyes upon that face:

And when her latest born doth ask
   What the deep sigh she heaveth meant?
The woman says, with quivering lips,
   "He was our President."

"But teacher told me of a score,—
   And almost all the names I know;—

And was not Washington the best,
    Who lived so long ago?"

Within the mother's eye a tear
    Rises, but doth not fall :—
"This was our martyred President—
    This face upon the wall."

Why, reader, was it in the hour
    Of doubt, distress and dread,
That such unbounded trust we felt
    In him, who, at the head,

Sat meek and gentle as a child
    Within the chair of state?
Was it the grace of noble birth?
    The statesman grand and great?

And, when across the continent
    His honored bier was borne,

What made the youthful and the old
   As for a father mourn?

Illini! land of men! no man
   Like him, so true and brave;
Whom thou, in our extremity,
   To head the nation, gave.—
None dear as he who sleeps to-day
   Within thine honored grave.

So dear to all—but dear the most
   To those, who, in our night of pain,
Uprose from slavery, a Host
   Long burdened with the shameful chain
Of mean oppression; rose and stood,
   One with the human brotherhood.

The hand that burst those bonds away,
   Now moulders into dust;
But world-wide honor gilds to-day

HOME.

The name of him who dare be just ;
The *man* in peril, Heaven sent—
 Our martyred President.

There is a place four turnpikes meet,
 The center of the town ;
A common, where the children play ;
 A green and rising mound :
It fronts the school, there children play—
 But 'tis a sacred ground.

There is a snow-white monument,
 That you may, any day,
See, as you enter into town,
 And see for miles away ;
And carved thereon are noble names,
 That never shall decay.

The aged, with uncovered head,
 Beside it come to kneel ;

And round and round, with steps of awe,
  The village maidens steal.
Look, stranger! in that list of names,
  Are James and Bruce McNiel!

YEARS AGO.

YEARS AGO:

A POEM OF THE ADIRONDACKS:

RETROSPECTIVE.

A few pale blossoms, plucked upon the lawn
Of early youth, and wound with autumn grass
And fallen leaves.

An ocean shell.
That beareth far in-shore the billows plaint:
A prisoned song-bird, ever trilling forth
One innocent love note.

An infant lost,
And buried by the redbreasts of the wood :
All that is pitiful, all that is pure ;
That bears upon its brow the dew of morn ;
That walks with upturned eyes earth's wilderness;
Or treads the heated share of martyrdom;
I fain would bring you in this song of mine.

Be it the withered grasses, or the shell ;
The faithful robin, or the fair, dead babe ;
Or just one thought : receive it in the name
Of Him who said, a sparrow falleth not
Without His eye.

A mountain—one of Adirondack's range :
Upon its sunrise slope, and half-way down,
Built round an iron mine, a village stands—
A little world away among the hills.
Above, the unfelled forest casts its shade

Adown the western side: and far beyond,
Upon its summit, sits a little lake,
Like infant fair upon its mother's breast,
Mirroring the fleece-clouds of an April sky;
Mirroring the purple thunder-storm;
The rose-light clustering about the dawn;
The night-queen, and the star-host, and the trees,
That round it clasp their green boughs lovingly;
And there the half-breed hunter fished and trap-
[ped:
And there were wigwams pitched upon its banks;
And o'er its waters glided bark canoes.

In heated seasons, men would hither come
From crowded city walks, and walls of brick,—
Of nature's wildness all enamored grown—
To hunt and fish, the whole long summer through:
With eyes that had been dimmed by midnight
[toil;
With brows untimely furrowed by thought;

With intellect a prey upon itself;
With cheeks that whitened in the commerce mart
Of mammon's dull and sombre counting-rooms;
And that disease which feeds on wasted hopes,
On broken hearts and half forgotten joys;
Would come and ask of those untrodden wilds
For solace, and for healing and repose:
And ever, if the wound was not too deep,
Kind Nature, that dear nurse who asks no fee,
Gave them a welcome and a speedy cure.

A road, like ribbon, girt the mountain's base,
And bound our mining village to the farms,
Where bronzed, hard-handed farmers, by their toil
Wrung from the rocky soil its scanty grain.
O, how unlike the vast yield of the West!—
God's fertile prairie-lands—that fill with ease
The meal-chests of the crowded Eastern world.
Skirting the forest-depths, a clearing stood:

There rang the woodman's axe all the day long;
There blackened stumps and ash heaps pointed
[out
The stubborn warfare tyrant man had waged
With Nature, in her own fortressed retreat;
How, Ishmael-like, his hand of greed is turned
'Gainst all the rest of God-created good:
He fells the oak; turns from its bed the stream;
Kills woodland song-birds, aye, from wantonness;
Out-crushes insect-life, for very sport;
Breaks down the briar-rose, then flings aside:
And not the ocean, on its coral bed;
And not the quarry, with its rocky heart;
And not the subtle properties of air;
Or the magnetic chain that binds the earth;
Or the volcanic fires that rage within,
But feel, or soon shall feel, his power of will.

When shone the suns of April; and the snow,
Melted from mountain top and mountain side,

A thousand rivulets come dancing down,
Shining and sparkling like a diamond shower,
With mystic music-song through every dell.
I never stand where waters gush along,
But they do tell me tales of long ago,
And bring me heart-aches over buried joy;
Then shadowy hands do come and clasp my own;
Then echoing tones of death-hushed voices steal
Into my heart; and summer eyes look down
From every cloud, till thrills of mem'ry bend
And shake me, like the frail reeds at my feet.

Between the clearing and the village, stood
My mother's cottage—an old-fashioned house—
Embowered in the apple-orchard shade.
In blossom season 'twas the sweetest place
I ever saw, or e'er expect to see:
Behind the house, abruptly rose a hill;
From out the hill-side gushed a tiny spring;

From thence, a little streamlet, falling down,
Passed by the house and crossed the field beyond;
The dashing song upon its pebbly bed,
Mixed strangely with dream-music as I slept,
Was the first melody that greeted morn.

My father, a shareholder of the mine,
Brought his young bride, in their first wedded
[days,
To that sweet cottage on the mountain side;—
There, all secluded from the outer world,
A world of bliss they found between themselves.

Well I remember the first shadow, flung
Like pall of darkness, o'er that sunny spot:—
Our youngest pet, Louisa was her name,
From school returned, a little wan and sad,
As if presentiment of her coming fate
Forecast its shadow on the darling's brow.
She took her little testament, to learn

A Sabbath lesson for the week to come ;
Twas all about the " Babe of Bethlehem."
That time-worn treasure lies before me now—
No gilt-bound oracle, or costly gift,
Has ever been so treasured in my heart.

How shall the dreariness that fell be told ?
She, tiny pail in hand, went to the spring :—
No more I saw her, till, upon the brink,
All drenched and cold, she, like a dead lamb, lay:
That night of terror shakes me even now :—
This was my first great sorrow, and it came
Before my heart had strengthened for its load.
Years never bring oblivion of the past ;
Though time, with rubbish, covers o'er the heart,
Old wrinkled scars and wounds, half healed, re-
[main,
That sometimes, by their aching, bring us back
The anguish-hours endured so long before.

RETROSPECTIVE.

There came a time, when deep unlifted gloom
Closed down like night around our hearts and
[home,
Out-shutting all the sunshine from our lives,
And blighting all green leaves and fragrant flow-
[ers.
There came a time, when only faith had power
To lift us from the sadness of the tomb;
When orphan tears fell like unwearied rain;
When widowed lips, with speechless grief, were
[dumb.
Mangled and crushed, they bore him from the
[mine,—
Without a warning and without a word,
The parting kiss still warm upon his lips.
Still, through the eastern lattice, shone the sun;
Still hung the dew, like jewels, on each shrub,
When came the crash that filled our hearts with
[woe;—
And then, another gray, unsodded grave:
Within our home, hushed tones and breaking
[hearts;
Within our lives, a tear-page blotted o'er.

Our Edward and our Eleanor were twins:
As like in infancy as two bright buds
Upon one stem—could scarce be told apart.
The same brown eyes, the long and silken lash;
The same short curls of golden-tinted brown.
When, hand in hand, the children trudged to
[school,
A stranger could have told that they were twins;
But as this child-age merged into the years
Of promise, of development, and prime,
There came a change; for Edward's took the form
Of manhood's vigor, nobleness, and strength;
And Ellen's form was rounding into grace.
The short, brown curls, lay thick on Edward's
[brow;
But Ellen's grew a massive, waving coil.
His eyes had still their frank, straightforward
[look;
Hers, drooped in sweet timidity and love.
Still were they much alike in heart and life;

For both were brave, and earnest, and most
[true.
Their mother's prop they stood in her lone hour;
For, when she found her means of life withheld,
And but a pittance left of all our wealth,
The children left their school-life and came home,
Willing to toil, nor did we see a tear;
Lifting life's burden on without a sigh;—
The blessing and the sunlight of our home.

Midway between the twins and cherub child,
So soon to heaven translated, I was born,
With nothing of my elder sister's grace,
Or rosebud loveliness of her who died.
It seemed to me I could do nothing well,
But only think, and *think*, e'en from a child:—
Yes, I could love with such intensity,
That all my inner being throbbed to pain.
With unclosed eyes, long night-hours would I lie,

Fearing the loss of those to whom I clung:
In dreams, I passed the star-gates to that home—
That upper home, beyond all parting pain;—
Pressed upward by the longing that I felt—
Longing and loneliness that would not cease.
When our dear father died, this loneliness
Was far more terrible for me to bear.
Oft through the silence came his tender voice;
Oft bent his face above me in my sleep;
Oft did I wake, his kiss upon my lips:
And no more did I doubt he came to me,
Than I did doubt he loved me while he lived.
O, how I loved the beautiful! and watched,
With hunger-eyes, my elder sister's face,
And turned away in bitterness and tears.
I would have given all the world to be
As joyous and as beautiful as she.
I could not play, as happy children play;
Nor could I tell the reason to myself,
That gentle, gleeful voices of the young

Should cloud my brow with discontent and gloom.
'Twas often said, "Sarah must go to school;"
But mother pleaded I should not be sent.
I think she understood me best of all ;
I think she wept above me secret tears ;
I think she trembled for me in her heart ;
I think she gladly would have folded
In her kind mother arms all my life long.

I cannot tell when first I learned to pray ;
'Twas further back than memory can reach :
I cannot tell when first I loved the Lord,
And thought of Him with still, adoring awe.
No more I doubted His existence, than
I did my own, and sometimes not as much :
For oft, in musing hours, I lost myself,
And merged my life in blossoms, rocks, and
[trees ;
Dreaming away long hours among the hills.
Those days, they were not happy, and not sad,

But something like the twilight, or the dawn ;—
Only they brought me neither day nor night,
But wrapped my still lips like a phantom spell.

That spell is broken now ; that dream-life fled :
And, looking back, I wonder at the child ;—
For scarcely does it seem that it was I.
I know there are some heart-lives most akin
To Nature's subtle influence and laws :
There is a kind of intuitial soul,
Like harp Æolian, played by hands unseen ;
And like Æolian music—mournful, sweet,
But fitful ; strange ; now breathing soft and low;
Now rising to discordant anguish-tones :—
If voice be granted such, they do become
The poets, prophets of their time and age ;
Their thoughts of beauty will not, cannot die :
Their life-songs echo down the passing years :
Their words of flame live on, through ages—on !

But some there be who never find a voice ;

Whose imaged beauty-visions lie entombed

Within the soul that formed them, ne'er brought
[forth ;

Or, clothed with words, go out into the world:

And there be poet-spirits, meanly clad

In fleshly garments, so no one beholds

The rare thought-jewels that are hidden there,

Like fountain bordered round by noxious weeds,

Which, shutting out the sunlight and the stars,

Hide its cool waters from the traveler,

Who doth, upon its brink, lie down and die.

Not always doth the soul look from the eyes ;

Or beams in smiles the heart-life on the lips.

Some noble natures that might bless the earth,

Like unused metals, do corrode and rust.

O, 'tis the talent hidden, bringeth woe !—

Fond mother do not ask it for thy child :

O, soul pray not that it be granted thee !

LUCRECE.

One bright June day a missive came to us,
For Edward, post-marked from a Southern town:
As brother told us,—from a college mate,
Who felt with failing health, the need of rest.
Might he, and his young sister, come awhile,
And nestle in our home-nest, 'mong the hills?
For, though they had great wealth at their com-
                                       [mand,
They had no parents—therefore had no home.
Sister Lucrece was wearied with the whirl
Of city life, and much desired this change:

He wrote that all their family were gone;
That both their parents died in the same year.
They two in this wide world were all alone.
The slow, sure plague that swept away their
[friends,
Had fixed on him its firm, unyielding grasp:
And he was weary now, from morn till night:—
He wanted, most of all, a loving home—
A quiet place, to gather strength, or die.

Anon they came. Truly upon his brow
The seal of death, thus early, had been set:
His eyes had caught a far-off look, as if
His thoughts and heart-hopes centered not on
[earth:
Upon his burning cheek, the long, dark lash
Drooped wearily; and, as he laid him down
Upon the snowy couch we had prepared,
He drew my mother's hand within his own,
And whispered, "Be my mother for awhile;—
The little while God gives me leave to stay."

And with him came Lucrece, a blooming girl,
On whose bright brow had twenty summers
[shone;
On whose round cheek was still the rose of health;
And she was tall and stately; full in form:
Back from her brow, her black, abundant hair
Was woven, in a shining, regal braid;
And she had great black eyes, and sweet, red
[lips;
A step as firm and proud as any queen:
So still, so graceful, and so self-possessed,
That I, at first, was half afraid of her;
But, when my mother came and took her hand,
There crept a wistful longing in her eyes,
And all their brightness melted into tears.

One evening, as the twilight folded back
Its bright flame-tinted curtains from the sky,
And hushed the world to let her darlings rest;
I leaned half out the casement: still as death

She came and stood beside me for a while,
Her lily hand upon my own, she said:
"What are you thinking, all alone, my child?"
"I do not know," I answered dreamily;
"I'm keeping silence with the silent night."
She bent her head, until its shining braid
Did rest upon my own, and whispered low—
"Will Sarah be my sister and my friend?—
I always thirsted for a sister's love.
When Willie dies, as die I know he will,
What friend or comforter have I on earth?"
Forgetting all my bashfulness, I turned
Impulsively, and clasped her round the neck;
And, from that eve, the influence she wove
About me strengthened as the days wore by.

Still, she was not familiar with the rest:
Some things I noticed gave me real pain:—
It seemed to me that she could never bear

The searching of a frank, straight-forward look:
She never bowed at morn or evening prayer.
Oft Willie's eyes were fixed upon her face,
And then they wore a sad, appealing look:
The death-white shadow of a pain intense,
Would lay for hours upon his still, fair face.
Once mother came, and, sitting by her side :—
"You do not kneel with us, my darling child;
Have you no love for Christ within your soul?"
She started up, and, then a little pale :—
"I have no love for one I do not know;
Your Christ is not my God, for I have none."

My mother turned away, without a word;
I shook, with awful fear, from head to foot.
There seemed to rise a plague-spot to her brow:
Those awful words seemed written there—"No
[God!"
I stood and looked upon her, from afar :

I did not speak to her all that day long.
She sat at her embroidery all that day :
She neither smiled nor spoke: her set face wore
A look of bitterness and cold resolve.
Slowly the day wore onward to its close.
Not always, when God bids His children rest,
Doth hush the heart its throbbing ; doth the brow
Cease aching, or the fevered pulse grow cool.

I sat me down, where smiled the hillside spring
Within its pebbly basin, all alone.
I watched the stars outcoming one by one,
And thus I thought : " He looks into our lives,
To see reflected glory like His own :"
And then I whispered, o'er, and o'er, and o'er :
"Without Hope, and without God in the world!"
Then threw myself upon the sod and wept.
How long I lay and wept, I could not tell.
A cold, damp hand fell heavy on my brow :

A whisper, hoarse and loud in its dismay—
"Dear little Sarah, am I lost to you?"
I pulled her down beside me, whispering,
"Darling Lucrece! O, do believe in God;—
He is so high, so holy, and so pure!"
"What do you know of Him?" in quick reply.
"I know what has been written in His book."
"His Book, poor child; the world is full of
                                    [books;
And I have one I'd like for you to read.
I found in my dead father's library,
Among the rubbish hid, a famous book;
The work of some old wise philosopher;
And all about the origin of things—
Air, earth, and minerals, and hidden fires.
Now, Sarah, if you're sure you're not afraid;
And, like our mother Eve, desire to know,
I have it here, and you shall read—my book;
But tell me first, if you have ever felt
What some do make so much of—that your sin
Is all forgiven you, for Jesus' sake?"

Alas, Lucrece! I never have, although
Dear sister Ellen and my brother have,
But I believe in Him with all my heart;
And then, you see, I am not like the rest,
Not half so wise and good, not half so strong.
I know I ought to consecrate my life,
I scarce can tell what makes me put it off:
I surely shall some day—I must, I *must!*
Give me your book, Lucrece; I'm not afraid
To learn all I may learn—and now, good-night."

WITHOUT GOD.

Silent and empty was our large old room,
Still glowed a little fire within the grate,
Because our evenings on the mountain-side,
Even in summer-time, were somewhat chill.
My father's easy-chair upon the hearth
Had been re-cushioned for the invalid,
My mother's work-stand by the window stood
And some half-finished garment lay thereon,
And other chairs were round a table drawn,
The dear old Bible, open at the place
Of evening lesson—these words met mine eye:

I read, "Lead us not into temptation."
O, silent warning from the *friend* of friends,
Like hand of love, when stray presumptuous feet
On danger's brink; well had it been for me
Had heed been given in that trial hour.
I stooped and pressed my lips upon the page,
With reverent care I closed the Holy Book,
Unclasped the other and sat down to read.

Upon its first page was a pictured face—
An old, old face, with broad, o'erhanging brow,
Deep, well-like eyes, that seemed instinct with
[life,
A mouth hard-closed and set with discontent,
While charnel whiteness seemed to cover all,
So full of strength, so shadowed o'er with woe,
So scornful, yet so earnest in its woe,
It wrung from me a shudder and a sigh.
I will not write the venomed lies that ran

Through the cursed pages of that awful book:
Its subtle reasoning,—Lucrece had said,
'Twas all about the origin of things;
But through, and through, this was the teaching [still—
No God, no God in all the universe,
That everything was governed by fixed laws
Immutable as destiny; it said,
Man's soul was like the spirit of the beast
That goeth downward into nothingness,
New life was resurrection, and our dust
Sought out new forms of life continually;
Religion was a myth of ages past,
Kept up by priests and churchmen to deceive.
All this was interwoven with such skill,
And made to look so plausible, my faith,
Unpropped by actual experience,
Straightway began to totter to its fall.

At first, I wept above my ruined hope,
And strove with frantic zeal to build again—
Amid the blackness grasped and groped to find
The old foundation stones; but sliding earth
Admonished, I had built upon the sand.
Then I grew desperate, but still read on,
Unwinding serpent coils of reasoning,
Cursing my mind that drank the deadly draught;
Cursing my hand that held the fatal book;
Cursing my heart because it did not break,
As my great Universal Sun went down.
I glanced around: God's Oracle was closed,
My paradise of pure belief was lost,
And all untasted the fair Tree of Life.

Chilled to the heart and spell-bound, on and on,
Unwinding all the serpent-coil of thought;—
The embers faded out within the grate,

The crescent moon went down behind the clouds,
Great pitchy banks upon the western sky;
The night-wind moaned among the mountain
 [pines—
As changed my heart-hopes so had changed the
 [night.

Still gave my candle its poor feeble light,
Like reason's fitful glow when faith is dead:
Spell-bound I sat and read and wept, and read
Until the serpent-coil was all unwound,
The death-charm woven and the ruin wrought.
Thus one, with soul long gone to its reward,
Could fetter other victims for the pit
In torture-bands of bitter unbelief:
The poison seeds *he* flung upon the breeze,
Wind-borne across the ocean and the land,
Sank in the untilled soil of my young heart
To ripen into fruit of sin and death.

O, it is well Jehovah hath delayed
His judgment sentence till the last great day;—
For, not until the Great White Throne be set,
Until the angel on the sea and land
Doth swear that time—frail time—no more shall
[be,
And man's probation ended, will that soul
Know the full measure of his cup of woe;
Not till the last soul-vessel hath gone down
In ruin by the influence he raised,
Until, that still increasing, widening wave,
Break on the rocks of God's eternal coast,
Can it be known the mischief he hath wrought.
Alas, for those whom he hath led astray!
Alas, alas, for that undying soul!
For his shall be " The worm that dieth not,"
And his "The fire that never shall be quenched!"

" Why fall so soon?" does one in wonder ask;
" Can thus the teaching of a life be turned

In one short hour to settled unbelief?"
I entered heedlessly the tempter's path,
And, grieved, the Spirit of my God withdrew.
And through the wilderness, I trod alone.
This know I: Fallen nature, unrenewed,
Doth bring forth weeds of evil speedily:
And this I know, for it was even so,
My poor sand-founded temple was no more:
The tempest came; the cold rain beat and beat;
My poor sand-founded temple was no more.

Shivering with cold, and miserable,
I crept into the room where Ellen lay
In slumber, peaceful as a rosy child's,
And deep; for she was wearied by the task
Of dear home duties, lovingly performed.
How pure in perfect rest she, smiling, lay!
Her bible, open, on the little stand,
Near by a chair, whereon she sat to read.

From habit-force I knelt beside the bed :
Whispered, " Our Father," then rose up again :
Muttered, in bitterness, " There is no God ;"
But O, I wish, I *wish* that it was true !"

Shivering with cold, and miserable,
I lay me by my sleeping sister's side :
It seemed to me I ne'er could sleep again ;
For, through my brain, dark visions of unrest
Kept whirling, shifting, jeering all the while :
But, when a faint light deepened in the east,
With promise of the day, I fell asleep.
In dreams, I knelt beside my father's grave,
And laid a wreath of violets thereon ;
And filial tears, like dew-gems, weighed each leaf.
Between me and the sun, that old, old face,
Smiling in wrath and bitter scorn, appeared :
A hand of ice raised me upon my feet :
A low, deep voice exclaimed, "Thou art a fool !

Thou hast no father, as thou hast no God;—
See! Thy earth-parent is but crumbling bones!"
Then opened wide the grave: I only saw
A few white bones; a handful of damp mould.
'Poor foolish dreamer!" cried the taunting voice;
"Cast all your withered blossoms in the tomb:
Soon, *very soon*, ye shall be like to him."

I woke. A cool hand lay upon my brow:—
"Dear little Sarah, you are ill to-day."
O, precious mother! How I longed to lay
My head upon her breast, and tell her all!
Alas! That there was written in my life,
For the first time, a page she might not read!
I only said, in tears, "My head does ache;
I do not wish to breakfast with the rest."

That afternoon, Lucrece came smiling in,
With bounding step, and glad, unconscious face:

With roses she had gathered in her walk,
Came in, and laid her roses on my bed.
I started up; and every quivering nerve
Strung to its utmost tension, by despair,
I beckoned her to take her roses hence :—
" Go, go, Lucrece! You've robbed my heart of
                                          [hope—
All hope of this life, and the life to come!
O, is it so? Is there no life to come?
Shut down, hemmed in, to this sin-darkened sphere!
Lucrece, you've robbed me, robbed me of my
                                          [soul!
Though it was but delusion, O, I wish
   The Bible and its promises were true!"

" I have not robbed you, Sarah," she replied;
" Is it not always best to know the truth?
Your peace was all unreal; it was like
   The smiling of an infant in its sleep."
" Then would you wake it up, because it smiled?

And is the whole enlightened world asleep?—
The 'Golden City,' is it but a myth?
The 'Tree of Life,' a fable? 'The Judgment
[Throne,'
We thought immutable, eternal, but a lie?
And is there nothing stable, nothing true,
That we may hang our hopes and hearts upon?
I've read of prisoners in dungeons kept
Till death; then buried 'neath the cold stone floor:
And, in derision, smiled, because I thought
The disembodied soul could not be barred.
This unbelief shuts out all life and joy—
Entombing soul and body in the dark!

My father lost! I thought him living still.
My buried sister—she is lost to-day.
And is it so? There is no Son of God,
No Christ!—This is the sorest loss of all.
Lucrece, what matters it how soon I die?—

Nay, if by mine own hand I take this life,
It were no sin, I'd rather die than live ;
But, O, my mother ! Let her still rejoice :
I'd rather die than ruin her belief :
One look from brother Edward's searching eyes,
Would filch its secret from my burdened heart ;
While, if I died some strange, mysterious way,
They would, in time, to it be reconciled,
And think swee thoughts of angel Sarah then,
When bloom the summer blossoms o'er my
 [grave."
All this I said in sorrow's monotone ;—
The dreary level accents of despair.

All Lucrece's color fled ;—she grew as white
As was the dress she wore: she tried to speak,
But, for a while, her voice was choked by sobs,
And drowning tears, and self-accusing grief :—
" Sarah, what can I say to comfort you ?"
" Lucrece, there is no comforter on earth ;

There is no hope. If we did but believe
In Christ, that were a sure relief:
If Christian faith be false, it is most sweet;
If it be dream, 'tis dream most beautiful.
Here, take your dreadful book!—Go, bury it
So deep, no mortal shall behold it more;
Let this poor world believe its better fate;
Let wounded hearts take comfort in their Christ;
Let mothers think their dead babes are alive;
And riven souls expect to meet again:
Let poor, down-trodden victims think there is
A Throne of justice, uncorruptible.
The child of poverty and wearing want,
Believe in Heaven's plenteousness and peace.
I'd rather nevermore behold the sun,
Than quench the faith-light of a single soul."

For weeks, that cloud of gloom hung o'er my
                                                       [life;
But, very skillfully, did I evade

The questioning my altered aspect wore,
While brooding daily on the thoughts of death;
For it was night and day upon my mind,
To find some way that no one would suspect
The work had been accomplished by my hand.
If other thoughts, than just the one of self,
Had found an entrance to my morbid soul,
I surely should have wondered at Lucrece,
Grown suddenly so silent and so sad;
And often, in the morning, did her eyes
Look red with weeping, or with watching, which
I could not tell; and she would read for hours
To Willie, in my mother's testament.
She read, but in a weary, absent tone,
As 'twas a penance placed upon herself:
At times, some sweet, kind words of Christ,
                          [would bring
The shining tears into her downcast eyes;
At times, His solemn warning pale her brow,
Or shake her, like the wind, with sudden dread;

But, mostly, she was self-possessed and calm.
I sometimes thought, as she did not believe,
What room was there for tenderness or fear?

My mother, more than usually you find
In women of this day, had sterling sense;
A heart, love-trained; a cultivated mind;
A faith, unwavering that had led her through
Affliction's trial-furnace, all unscathed:
No weak and faltering disciple, she
Walked firmly, uncomplainingly, with God,
Rejoicing in the spring-time and the flowers;
Rejoicing in the night-shade and the storm;
No timid, half believer of His Word;
Though versed in science, mother always made
Her Oracle of life, the Book of God.

One day said Edward: "What can ail the girls?
For sister is so gloomy and morose;

And all the time Lucrece appears so sad.
They do not walk together as they used.
Can they have quarreled? O, what can it be?"
Then mother said: "My boy, I do not know;
I fear Lucrece has poisoned Sarah's mind.
To-morrow is the Sabbath; let us make
That day, a day of fasting and of prayer:—
Pray for your sister; pray for poor Lucrece:
You know, where two agree, what Jesus said,
It should be granted, let us go to God."
Thus was our house divided 'gainst itself;
Thus was the force of evil and of good
To deadly conflict brought; the price—a soul.
Ah! Little did I know that summer morn
The league of prayer before His mercy throne,
That said to powers of evil in my soul;
Said to the darkness overwhelming me—
"Thus far thou mayest, and no further, go!"

THE WILDERNESS.

Still walked I in the gloom ; though in God's [mind

The dawn had been created, even now.

The tempter's final trial hour had come—

The day that I, in desperation, said

Should be my last ; for no one hath the right

To bid me live, when I desire to die.

There is not happiness enough on earth

To overbalance all of human ill ;

Justice enough, to recompense the wrong :

And, since there be no future for the soul ;

No retribution,—aye, and no reward,
It never can be sin to lay it down.
What love is strong enough to bind me here,
To suffer through long years, and then grow old?
We mourned Louisa, just a little while—
We scarcely miss the darling from our midst—
But think of her as living in the light.
Dear mother! She will have one care the less;
And Edward, one the less to labor for.
Sweet Ellen!—But I have not been, of late,
So sisterly she need to mourn for me;
Lucrece will drink the bitterest cup of all,
But there will be one comfort, e'en for her—
Since, not believing that I have a soul,
She will not fear, or fancy, mine is lost.

And so the little taper light that shone
So fitful and so feebly, will go out:
This throbbing heart, these busy hands, will make

Fit nourishment for other forms of life ;—
Maybe the roots of some fruit-bearing tree,
Shall, reaching down, invade my resting place ;
And, sucking up the juices from my mould,
Through all the veins and life-cells of the trunk,
Change me to bud, and green, unfolding leaves ;
Maybe a thousand blades of grass or grain,
Will draw their vital nourishment from me,
And, drinking in the sunshine and the dew,
With golden wealth make glad the heart of man.

Northward from us, upon the mountain side,
Long years before, a mine had been commenced,
Then given over for its present site,
Now overgrown with briars, till it seemed
A great, black cavern, opening in the earth.
Thus had I thought : Should I, some day, be
                              [missed ;
Should I be found dead here, among the rocks,
And withering wild flowers scattered all around,

They'd think I lost my footing and fell in:—
Lucrece, I know, would never dare to tell.

That Sabbath morning, all the earth did seem
Fair as forbidden Eden, as I gazed
Adown the wooded valley, o'er the fields,
Across a distant lake, upon the spires
Of one fair city in another State,
The gold of sunrise, first upon the spires,
And then the lower hills ; and then the plain,
All broken into farms ; and, last of all,
The lowlands, following the river banks,
Green with its belt of forest, all the way :—
This was my world; this, from my infant years,
Had grown familiar as my mother's face ;
But ne'er, before I stood to look farewell,
Drank I its beauties, as I did that morn.
I strove to hush the rising of my sobs,

Lest some familiar sound should be unheard;
And crowded back the tears, that I might see,
With far-stretched vision, every sight I loved.

I pleaded illness, and remained at home.
Alas! How like a traitor did I feel,
As sister kissed me, ere she went away;
The bitter cry that rose upon my lips;
The deep heart-wail I smothered to a sigh,
And struggled, as we sometimes do in dreams,
From which, strive as we may, we cannot wake.
The tolling of the Sabbath bells grew still;
The footsteps of my dear ones died away:
I hushed my heart, and, with deep calmness, said:
"Now is the bitterness of death all passed!
Who is there, on this earth, that hath the right
To bid me live, when I desire to die?"

I stood at Willie's door, and then went in:
"What is it, little Sarah? You look ill.

Thanks be to God for this sweet day of rest:
Dear child, cast all your care upon the Lord."
His loving words o'ercame me, and I wept:—
A strange, quick impulse seized me, and I bent
And kissed his brow, and, whispering, said
["good-bye."

That Sabbath day, within the lonely wood,
Did Willie's words keep ringing in my ears—
"Thanks be to God for this sweet day of rest:
Sarah, cast all your care upon the Lord."
I said: "Because there is no Christ, no God,
To care for me, therefore I will not live:
Because the bright belief of childhood's days
Is lost for aye, therefore *I will not live:*
There's naught below that can compensate
For such a loss, therefore I will not live."

Then, as I walked and pulled the woodland
[flowers,

I said: "What is my life worth more than [these,
If there be not a soul within this clay?
True, I have power to act, and think, and feel;—
How do I know but these are just the same?
How do I know, as I break down this rose,
But conscious life goes out? How do I know?
Can other forms of life experience
This intense longing, and this drear unrest?
We must have something strong to lean upon;—
We can no more stand upright than the vine:
Because there is no pure and Holy One
To hold me up, I cannot bear to live;—
And you, wild flowers, lie with me in the dark;
I am your sister, though not half so fair."

Thus murmuring to myself, I went along,
Until I reached the black mouth of the pit:
Then I looked down and shuddered; I was young;

And O, that morning was so very fair;
And Willie's gentle words rang in my ears:—
"Dear child, cast all your care upon the Lord."
The demon spirit that had led me on
To my destruction, was not yet cast out;
A cloud of gray obscured the noonday sun:—
It said: "Do not you see how earth good fades?
How summer ends in autumn's dismal storm?
How buoyant youth must merge in dreary age?
See all your blossoms wither!—They are dead:
And you, their sister, are afraid to die."

I went, and stood upon the black pit's edge;
And said: "O, Earth! I bid you not adieu;
I come to rest me in your loving arms."
Just then I heard a hasty step, and felt
Two arms about me, and a rain of tears
Upon my face—then consciousness was gone.

When it returned, I lay in Lucrece's arms;

My cheeks wet with her tears; upon my brow

Was pressed her lips; and in her soft warm
[hands,

My own, all icy cold, were tightly held;

I started wildly up: "You have no right

To keep me here; nor do you dare to tell!"

She held me close: "Dear Sarah, you have
[dared

To break your mother's and your sister's heart:

I tell you, Sarah, I will dare to tell;

For, should they curse, it cannot add one pang.

You will not listen?—Then we both will go,

And, at your mother's feet, confess the whole;

Or sit you hear, and I will tell you all;

And, when you hear, you surely will forgive."

"Lucrece; the God in whom I once believed

Would not forgive, if I did not forgive;—

But, as there is no God, I am not bound."

"Now, hear me, Sarah : surely as the sun
Doth shine upon the earth, there is a God !
And, as I do believe, truly I fear
That I have sinned the sin that's unto death ;—
For pray I cannot ; and the very sky
Seems brass above my head. Not for myself ;
But, darling, I have tried to pray for you.

I was about your age when sent to school,
From mother's care and guiding voice away ;
An inexperienced child, exposed
To chance direction, be it good or ill ;—
A school where brilliant gifts and intellect
Ranked higher than the graces of the heart.
I, for its highest honors, would compete,
And set my rank-mark second unto none :
There first I lost child-innocence and trust ;
For days and weeks passed by without a prayer:

There I imbibed the fatal fallacy,
That unbelief gives evidence of strength.

So, when the sorest trial of my life
Recalled me, filled with anguish, to my home,
I was not able to endure the cross.
I saw my mother, patient as a saint,
Grow weaker, sweeter, holier, every day;
Then, in those bitter hours, I went to God—
Went pleading for my precious mother's life:—
Pleading and striving, as if strife could stay
A ripened spirit from its upper rest.
I said: if Thou wilt spare her, I'll believe.
Thus made I controversy with my God.
She soon beheld the face of Him she loved.
She passed in peace not knowing my resolve—
My firm resolve, that never, never more,
Would I ask aught of Him, or own my God!

I saw my father die, without a prayer;
I never asked that Willie might be spared:—
The Lord could do as pleased Him, with His
 [own;
And, though I walked the earth without a
 [friend,
I did resolve that I would never yield.
But, Sarah, this sweet home-life breaks my heart—
I feel so like a serpent in the nest:
Though, for myself, I have not dared to come,
I've bowed in dust before Him—plead for you.
I would give all the world, to find some one
Of perfect faith, and pure, love-burdened heart,
Who knew me not, and yet would pray for me!"

"Lucrece," I said, with cold and cynic tone,
" It seems to me you have changed wondrous
 [soon ;—
'Till you can answer those wise arguments
Of that old book you were so free to lend,
I tell you plainly, I will not believe!

But, if you wish to find unwavering faith,
Then come with me, and I will show you one
Who never doubted once in all her life ;
If there be such a thing as answered prayer—
You may depend upon it, her's will be."
Lucrece was truly humbled ; so we went.
I brought her to a cottage, where was found
A rare sweet saint, who had not left her bed
Through long, long years of patient suffering :
Who lived alone for Christ, day after day,
By weakness, perfected, in trust, complete.

That day she was alone. The Sabbath sun
Cast glory-rays upon her spotless bed.
Ne'er might she tread the consecrated aisles ;
But not more holy those hushed temple courts,
Than was the solemn peace of that still room.
We stood upon the threshold, and I said :
" Eunice ! Lucrece desires to talk with you."

Then sat me down before the open door.
Lucrece crept in, and stood beside her bed.
She said: "I'm sick of sin, and want to find
My way to Christ; but O, I am afraid
That I have wearied out Redeeming Love."
Eunice said quietly: "You think you're lost."
"I know I am." "Then do not you despair;
The Master came to seek and save the *lost!*"
"Eunice, I cannot pray; I find no words,
Although my heart is yearning for His love,
Until it almost breaks." "Pray with your heart,"
Said Eunice, "for God knows the heart—*your*
[heart."
"Alas! What offering have I to bring?"
"A broken and a contrite heart He'll not de-
[spise.
"Will not you pray for me? Will not you ask?"
"Yes, I will ask our Father—you believe."

And thus, while wondering at the once proud girl,
My heart all bitterness and unbelief,

Into the Kingdom, as a little child,

Washed by His blood, she entered, and found
[rest.

If anything could have convinced my mind,

Those arguments, unanswered, 'twas her face,

All bright with hope, joy-lit, and full of love ;

A timid look she wore, as if she trod

On holy ground ; and an uplifted gaze,

As if the Land of Life was opening wide

Its pearly portals : gentle as a child

She plead with me to make her peace my own.

"No," answered I ; "your mantle, unbelief,

I needs must wear; peace may not come to me;

It is no part of my inheritance."

Ye who are mothers, and have faith in God ;

Ye who have children, in the broad sin-way,

Unsheltered and unshielded, only know,

By your own prayers, how mother prayed for
[me.

All day her heart-cry went above for light,
To Him who lives in love's unclouded day;
Within her closet's sacred solitude
Her great prayer-struggle deepened into power;
And she, with her petition, boldly pressed
Into the presence-chamber of her King,
Then light broke forth: she knew that she was
    [heard;
And, going to a little cabinet,
She smiled, and took therefrom a time-worn
    [book—
A gift it was, from one whose hand was laid
Upon her brow, beside baptismal font.
" I needed not the reasoning," she said;
" But this, perhaps, may be an outstretched arm,
For the salvation of my darling child."

PEACE.

Meanwhile did Willie's feet press hard the brink
Of death's dark billows, waiting for the call:
Meanwhile dusk vapors, rising, half engulphed,
Half hid him, from the watchers by his side.
For long, long hours, he lay in still content:
Anon would rally, and speak thrilling words—
Such words as only they between two worlds—
The dying and the living—can command.

He said: "I hoped to hold aloft the Cross,
Proclaiming pardoning love to sinful man:—

The Master had another cross for me.
Edward, my brother, be upon *thy* heart
The glorious work my failing hands lay down;
Thine be my wealth;—for Jesus' holy cause,
O, let mine only earth-tie be thy care!—
It is enough; thou knowest my desire."
Then his cold fingers clasping mother's hand,
He said: "The orphan's blessing rests on thee."
He looked in Ellen's tearful eyes, and smiled:
" Ellen, if I had lived, I might have told
Another story in thine ears; but now,
All that is over :—dear, sweet girl, goodby."
He said: " Lucrece, I know thou art at rest
In the Beloved,—I read it on thy brow.
O, darling sister! 'Twas the Master's pledge,
He giveth, when He answereth our prayer.
I do not leave thee friendless: loving arms
Are all about thee, and a higher love
Out-weigheth all. I leave thee without fear."

"Now, little Sarah, by my side sit thou,
And watch, until the final hour shall come.
Thinkest thou this life-like taper will go out
In nothingness, when these clay walls come down?
I tell thee, Sarah, God, to dying eyes,
Gives intuitions others may not know.
I tell thee, Sarah, even now Christ's hosts
Are gathering—gathering all about my bed.
I see them, though earth sunlight groweth dim;
I hear their anthems, though your voices fall
But dull upon mine ears. Well know I now
How much Eternity outweigheth Time!"
Ah! Did he know upon his dying couch;
And did I know, as I sat silent there,
The first out-reaching of my youthful heart
Had claimed him, as the purest and the best.
Now, every fibre breaking, by the pain,
I knew it, as the death-veil fell between;
I knew it through long, lonely after years.

A great awe fell upon me, as I sat
And watched the death-tide in its ebb and flow;
And followed, with mine own, his upturned gaze;
Beholding visions unrevealed to me.
He met my look, and, pointing upward, smiled;
And once his voice came faintly wafted back,
As from a far-off distance, murmuring "Home."
Then he was gone. The pale, forsaken clay,
Like an abandoned cottage on the moor,
With doors and windows closed, and hearth-stone
[cold,
And sweet love-voices silent evermore.
They bore him back to his old childhood home;
Back to the meadows where, a boy, he played;
Back to the mansion his forefathers reared;
Into the room where first he saw the light.
And there old neighbors, for his father's sake;
Old friends and playmates gathered, for his own.
Returning "earth to earth," and "dust to dust."
Yet not alone went Lucrece with the dead;

Brother and sister visited her home,
To ward away her loneliness of heart.
Thus found she, as her sainted Willie said,
Fond arms around her—God's love everywhere.

In these, the saddest days of all my life,
My mother found the key that did unlock
My past heart-wanderings; and I told her all.
Among some cast-off things Lucrece had left,
We found the book of ruin: brought it forth;
And, in the garden, 'neath fruit-laden trees,
We read it over, mother and myself.
It was another thing beneath the smile
Of glorious daylight—God's sun overhead.
The same dark reasoning and subtle doubt;
The same fell purpose—but the spell worked not.
Christ and a mother's love its power annulled:
And then the little book, her pastor's gift,

Was studied, and a blessing lay therein—
A blessing to the mother and her child.
Faith, new-created in my heart, cried out:
"What hindereth thee from entering into rest?
So thou believe with all thy heart, thou mayest."
And, as we bowed in prayer, the Holy One
Came near, and placed his love-seal on my brow.

God giveth peace. He only, giveth rest.
To me, 'twas sweeter than the silvery spring,
When cliff, and rock, and burning, shifting sand,
The dreary sickness of a hope deferred,
Sink in the past, the dead past traveled o'er.
Thus hath my story ended, just as life—
The Christ-life of my heart—had been commenced.
Before that hearth-stone doth a stranger sit;
Around that hillside spring, glad children play.
Sweet Ellen left us in a little while;

She heard a cry, one solemn autumn night—
"Behold the Bridegroom cometh!" she arose
And trimmed her lamp, and went to meet her
                                        [God.
O, sister, many stars are in thy crown;
But mine adorns another diadem.

And, even now, I feel the loving touch
Of blessing hands, that fell upon my brow;
And, even now, when twilight hush comes down,
The thrill of golden words fall on mine ear,
That may not be forgotten. Mine inheritance
Grows strangely rich, with dear ones gone before;
For mother hath, at last, been summoned home.

But two of us remain by Edward's side.
A noble woman walks the path of life;
Her husband's heart doth softly in her trust;
Her children do arise and call her blessed.

PEACE.

Far, far above the rubies, is her price.
Her husband, when he sitteth in the gate,
Is known among the elders of the Lamb.

In truth, God's ways, to me, are wonderful—
All full of goodness, and past finding out!
While this great world moves on, I, in my heart,
Keep silence still before Him, and rejoice:
What my hand findeth, do I with my might:
What my heart feeleth, hide I in my heart.
I keep the Oil of Grace within my lamp;
For soon I hope to hear the Bridegroom's voice:
And I hope to be early at the feast.

LOVE AND YOUTH.

Sweetheart, the birds have come again!
Earth, loosened from the winter's chain,
Bares her fond breast to April rain.
Upon my memory, all day long,
Hath lain this burden of a song:
"Love conquers Time, for Love is strong."

What matter then the silver-gray,
Sweetheart, upon thy brow to-day?
For every line of thought and care

Is holy as the hour of prayer,
While still unfolds this bud of truth;
Love bears the palm, for "Love is Youth."

Age, with his mantle, cold and white,
May hide the vernal heart from sight;
Yet, through the long, bright days of spring,
Sweet violets keep blossoming,
And summer song-birds sing this song:
"Love conquers Time, for Love is strong."

LOYAL.

Loyal to friend and lover;
   Clear as the furnace gold;
Stooping to falsehood, never;
   Too pure to be bought and sold:
His word, as his bond, unquestioned;
   Living a life so true;
Free from all tricks in trading—
   Can this be said of you?

In the day of his country's danger,
   He marched to the battle-field,

Seeking no high commission,
  Scorning the base word—yield ;
Willing to carry the musket ;
  Willing to wear the blue ;
Willing to die, if need be—
  Can this be said of you ?

Loyal to his Creator ;
  Defying the siren, Sin ;
Engaging the hosts of Satan,
  With a zeal that is sure to win :
He will never lay off the armor,
  Fighting the whole fight through ;
Loyal to his Creator—
  Can this be said of you ?

THE LOST.

In his country's halls of Congress,
  With a giant step he trod;
And the people listened to him,
                As a god.

As the fierce tornado sweepeth
  Through the forest oaks its way,
So the great heart of the nation
                He could sway.

He was wise among the wisest;
  He was strongest of the strong,

When he hurled his fierce invectives
                'Gainst the wrong.

But I saw his strength departed—
  He had paid the fearful cost;—
He had listened to the tempter:—
                He was lost!

Like a wreck upon the ocean,
  Weather-bound and tempest-toss'd,
He went down amid the darkness:—
                He was lost!

*   *   *   *   *   *

Her step had all the lightness
  Of the timid, graceful fawn;
And her eye had caught the brightness
                Of the dawn.

Like the fragrant water-lily;
  Like the daisy of the wild,

She was pure and unsuspecting
As a child.

But a fiend, clothed like an angel,
 The maiden's pathway crossed,
And he lured her to destruction :—
She was lost !

Like the broken water-lily,
 By the tempest torn and toss'd;
Like the daisy, crushed and trampled :—
She was lost !

*   *   *   *   *   *

He was young, and strong, and hopeful;
 He was generous and fair;
But we heard his shriek of anguish
And despair !

Though we begged him not to enter;
  Though we plead the fearful cost,
He was lured upon the threshold :—
            He was lost!

And we heard the fiends rejoicing,
  And the demons shriek and yell,
As they led their poor chained victim
            Down to hell.

From the loving arms around him;
  From the altar and the cross ;—
In the gay saloon of pleasure,
            He was lost.

THE SINGER.

She sat in the door of a cottage small;
The people were thronging along that way;
We had gained a victory over the sea,
And this was a jubilant holiday.
The sun came out from behind a cloud,
And the little maiden began to sing;
Her voice was as sweet as the robin's call,
On the budded boughs of the early spring.

"Jesus, lover of my soul, let me to thy bosom
　　　　　　　　　　　　　　　[fly!"

THE SINGER.

An old man stood in the street below,
Jostled and crowded—he had lived too long;
And, heavily leaning upon his staff,
He list' to the words of the fair child's song.
Day after day, like a heavenly strain,
Those words kept coming, and coming again.

"Other refuge have I none; hangs my helpless
[soul on thee."
A woman passed by in a coach so grand,
With liveried driver, and footman tall;
But she lowered her veil with her jeweled hand.
Lest the people should notice the great tears fall:
And all day long, like a sweet refrain,
Those words kept coming, and coming again.

"Thou, O, Christ, art all I want, more than all
[in Thee I find."
An invalid leaned on his mother's arm:
His eyes were as deep as the dark, still night:

A mocking flame on his thin cheek burned,
Like a funeral candle's transient light.
Like the breezes of Eden, the sweet refrain
Kept coming and coming, and coming again.

" Plenteous grace with thee is found—grace to
                       [cover all my sins."
The ears of a Magdalene caught the strain,
And her lips of their curses grew strangely dumb;
She crept as near to the white-robed child,
As the lost to the ransomed dare to come.
Like the pleadings of mercy, the sweet refrain
Kept coming and coming, and coming again.

On the little grass plot by the cottage door,
Are the merry voices of children at play ;
But the song of the silvery-toned is hushed;
Under the blossoming daisies to-day,
Sometimes a Magdalene comes and bends

Over the blossoms, her brow so pale;
Sometimes the bride of a nobleman kneels
Down in the dasies, closely veiled.

"Jesus loves," the old man sings,
As he sits, and the shadows are growing long,
"Thou, O Christ," through the death room rings,
With the swell of an anthem, the victor's song.
The people come and the people go,
And the harps of their lives are with discord
[strung;
But, once in a while, God sends to earth
The soul of a singer forever young.

ROLL ON.

Roll on, O river, to the sea!—
   Roll on, and on!
My soul, to vast Eternity,
   Goes on and on!
And when at last the angels stand
Upon the sea, and on the land,
And swear that time no more shall be,
Thou shalt a thing forgotten be!—
O, river, what art thou to me—
Art thou to me?

Shine on, O moonbeams, cool and bright!—
   Shine on and on!
And flood the earth with borrowed light—
   Shine on and on!
But, when the hand of God shall roll
The clouded heavens like a scroll,—
And mine is vast eternity—
Thou shalt a thing forgotten be!—
Then what art thou, O moon, to me—
Art thou to me?

Wave on, O proud oak, tall and high!—
   Wave on and on!
And spread thy strong arms to the sky—
   Wave on and on!
But one small century is thine,
While vast eternity is mine.
I shall God's glorious kingdom see;

But thou, a thing forgotten be.
Then what, tall oak, art thou to me—
Art thou to me?

O, fair green earth, beneath my tread.
  Bloom on and on!
And hide the generations dead—
  Bloom on and on!
Uprising from their mighty tomb,
We shall behold thy fiery doom,
When thou shalt dust and ashes be!
Then what art thou, O earth, to me—
Art thou to me?

www.ingramcontent.com/pod-product-compliance
Lightning Source LLC
Chambersburg PA
CBHW021729220426

43662CB00008B/767